SUPREMACY
— *and* —
SURVIVAL

SUPREMACY *and* SURVIVAL

HOW CATHOLICS ENDURED THE ENGLISH REFORMATION

BY STEPHANIE A. MANN

Scepter

Published by Scepter Publishers, Inc.
P.O. Box 211
New York, NY 10018
www.scepterpublishers.org

ISBN: 978-1-59417-079-9

Printed in the United States of America

Cover Design: Eric Sawyer/Rose Design

Text Design: Carol Sawyer/Rose Design

To My Husband Mark,
Who Always Told Me I Should

— MARCH 2007

Contents

PART 1

THE TUDOR REFORMATIONS

PART 2

STUART REVOLUTIONS AND RELIGIOUS SETTLEMENTS FROM THE SEVENTEENTH CENTURY TO THE TWENTIETH

Illustrations

FOUND AFTER PAGE 92

St. Thomas More

Blessed Margaret Pole

Campion and Companions: Alexander Briant,
Edmund Campion, and Ralph Sherwin

Robert Southwell

St. Oliver Plunkett

Mary of Modena

Baring/Chesterton/Belloc: Maurice Baring,
Hilaire Belloc, and G. K. Chesterton

Richard Challoner

Introduction

IT TOOK ME THIRTY YEARS to write this book. My fascination with the Tudors and the Stuarts began in high school with historical novels about Henry VIII's six wives and the English Civil War. They displaced in my affections the Plantagenet family (Henry II and Eleanor of Aquitaine, the three Edwards, Richard the Lionheart, and Richard II) whose romances and family feuds I relished in Thomas Costain's novels and histories. With the Tudors and Stuarts, I studied not only their lives, but also their eras' literature and music (Shakespeare and Sidney; Dowland and Donne): naturally, I was an English major in college (with a minor in history).

While in college, I learned about John Henry Newman. After twelve years of Catholic school, I went to a state university in my hometown, joining the campus parish, the Newman Center. During my sophomore year, I attended a Newman School of Catholic Thought on the life, works, and influence of Cardinal Newman. Investigating his life, works, and influence led me to study the Via Media, which led me to study the Church of England and the English Reformation under the Tudor and Stuart kings and queens.

Even as academic studies in undergraduate and graduate school led me to investigate Jane Austen, classical and modern rhetoric, the Metaphysical poets and many other subjects, Cardinal Newman and the English Reformation remained constant interests.

Following Newman's advice to the laity of nineteenth-century England, I saw the English Reformation as the perfect opportunity to learn enough of Church history to be able to defend the Church, especially as historical revisionism began to chip away at the Whig interpretation of the Reformation's necessity and inevitability. Catholics in England had endured nearly three hundred years of persecution, martyrdom, and suspicion, yet Catholics today are barely aware of this history. There are at least three reasons why Catholics need to know more about the English Reformation.

First, Catholics need to know more about Church history in general. Non-Catholics often ask about famous or infamous events in Church history: the Galileo case, the Inquisition, the Crusades, and others. We need to be able to answer questions or respond to attacks with context and facts. The person asking or attacking probably doesn't have time to hear a long, scholarly explanation, but we should be able to tell her something that might remove some prejudice against the Church or at least make her think.

We are also used to hearing how corrupt the Church was before the Reformation, how Martin Luther brought Christianity back to the purity of the apostolic era. Under the influence of Enlightenment views, we may think of the Middle Ages as an era of darkness and superstition. According to that view, the Reformation (and the Renaissance) comes as renewal and freedom. We need to know the rest of the story—how much more complex the Reformation was in Europe. One way to learn more about this complex history is to understand the English Reformation.

Also, Catholics should know about the English Reformation because of all the fascinating people they will encounter. Martyrs like Thomas More, John Fisher, Margaret Pole, Edmund Campion, Margaret Clitherow, Robert Southwell, and Philip Howard model in an extraordinary manner the virtues of loyalty to the faith and dedication to the truth. The monarchs of the Tudor and Stuart era, including Oliver Cromwell, the non-royal Lord Protector, are not necessarily models of virtue, but they are complex human characters whose lives had tremendous impact on their country, not least because of the religious decisions they imposed on their subjects. Occupying a sort of middle ground are those subjects—who faced tremendous choices about whom to serve and why—like Thomas Wolsey, Thomas Cranmer, William Byrd, John Donne, George Calvert, and William Laud. We may not have the opportunity to be martyrs like More and Fisher, but we may not be able to avoid the frustrating dilemmas these men endured. Moreover, the Catholic converts of the nineteenth and twentieth centuries, from Newman and Manning to Chesterton and Anscombe, are certainly worth knowing.

Finally, there is the ecumenical reason. It is essential that we know the history of the conflict between the Church of England and the Catholic Church, not to redress old hurts, but to understand the source of current issues. If we don't acknowledge the truth of what happened, any effort to find unity will be artificial. When Pope Paul VI was about to canonize and beatify a large group of English Catholic martyrs, there were some who discouraged him, saying that it was not a good ecumenical gesture to bring up these martyrdoms. The pope proceeded with the canonizations in 1970 because he hoped that the blood of the martyrs would be able to heal the wounds of the English Reformation, looking forward to the time when the Catholic Church would be "able to embrace her ever beloved Sister in the one authentic communion of the family of Christ: a communion of origin and of faith, a communion of priesthood and of rule, a communion of the saints in the freedom and love of the Spirit of Jesus."[1] Since 1970, even if more obstacles have been placed in the way of this reunion, we still need to realize the truth of what divides us, so that we don't adopt some false and foolish unity.

The story of the English Reformation was once told according to a Protestant or Whig interpretation. The liberal Whig party was progressive and reforming, so the Whig historians saw the Reformation in England as a necessary step in the progress of liberal civilization. This view has faltered in recent years, and the new historical interpretation of the English Reformation is more complex. The English Reformation is different from those on the continent of Europe in the sixteenth century, as religious reformers, Luther, Calvin, Melancthon, or Zwingli, led them. The English Reformation was led by a king, not because of Church scandals or abuses, but because the pope would not grant him an annulment of his first marriage. There was no Johann Tetzel in England to shock an English Luther into protesting the sale of indulgences or the abuse of the doctrine of purgatory. Instead, there was a vibrant Christian community—not perfect, of course, but one that united the people in the celebration of the sacraments and the redeeming life and death of Jesus Christ through the liturgical year, integrated into their lives and their culture. The English Reformation did not need to happen because of an unreformed Church or a disgruntled populace.

The English Reformation, led by the king, was legislated and enforced by the secular government. Thus, state power was used to command religious uniformity, as everyone had to believe as the king believed. Henry VIII replaced the Pope as head of the Church of England, and dissolved his first marriage so he could remarry in his quest for a legitimate son and heir. Otherwise, he wanted to remain a Catholic. He did not want a Protestant form of worship, theology of salvation, or reliance upon individual scriptural interpretation. Throughout his reign, he enforced a more traditional Christianity— yet divisions remained. After his reign, the role of the monarch as the head of the Church created a confusing pattern of religious change. It must have been frustrating for the common person to have different religious legislation with each change in the Tudor succession. Only the longevity of the last Tudor monarch, Elizabeth I, created the stability to put the Church of England on stronger foundations—yet both Catholics and Puritans remained in opposition to the established church.

Thereafter, under the Stuarts in the seventeenth century, the Church of England suffered divisions between the High Church Anglicans and the Evangelical Puritans. Catholics suffered from the penal laws as they continued to practice their faith. With each change in regime, the government's Church of England dealt with diversity by legislating uniformity and supremacy.

This history of a state church provides citizens of the United States of America a contrasting model to our constitutional relationship between church and state. It might provide us with some insights into the wisdom of our founders, who rejected an official state church at the federal level and provided a foundation for tolerance of differences in religious practice.

This book will show from the theological or religious point of view that the English Reformation under King Henry VIII need never have happened. The history of the English Reformation is a story about power and, indeed, force, as the king and Parliament—and his heirs and subsequent Parliaments—set out to arrange Anglican Church structure, worship, and doctrine, based on a combination of religious and political motives. The practice of power and politics continues throughout the history of the Church of England, and the book will trace that legacy through the tumultuous Stuart age, including the interregnum of Oliver Cromwell's protectorate, and into the Hanoverian era. Throughout, special attention will be paid to those who dissented from the state-established Church of England, especially to the Catholics of England.

Part One focuses on the Tudor era. In chapter 1, we will see how the Roman Catholic Church in England on the eve of Henry's break from Rome was a strong community, with excellent lay involvement, efforts by bishops and theologians to improve the Church and remedy abuses, a vibrant monastic tradition, and a determined apologetic response—which included the king himself—against the Continental Reformers. Chapter 2 recounts the events that led Henry VIII to declare himself the head of the Church of England and to sever all ties with the Pope in Rome. We will see how Henry limited the Protestant character of the Reformation, denying the more Lutheran efforts of Thomas Cromwell and Thomas Cranmer to change the liturgy. In chapter 3, we focus on the reign of Edward VI, when the Protestant efforts in England, directed by the government, were more aligned to radical Calvinist or even Zwinglian theology of salvation and the role of the church. Mary's brief reign and the return of Catholicism to England will be addressed in chapter 4, while chapter 5 describes the final Tudor religious settlement, reached and enforced by Elizabeth I, including the recusancy laws against Catholics that led to the great Jesuit missions and martyrs throughout her reign.

In Part Two, we will examine the tumultuous history of the Stuart era. As chapters 6 and 7 describe, the ecclesiology of the Anglican Church developed more fully under James I and his son Charles I, while Catholics continued to be restricted and mistrusted. During the interregnum and protectorate, the Presbyterian leadership of Oliver Cromwell, his New Model Army, and Parliament triumphed over the Church of England until it was reestablished with the monarchy in the Restoration of Charles II. James II's efforts to alleviate discrimination against Catholics led to the Glorious Revolution in 1688 and the Parliamentary Settlement (chapters 7 and 8). As the Church of England declined during the Latitudinarian Enlightenment of the eighteenth and nineteenth centuries, efforts to revive its influence and effect in people's lives included the Methodist and the Tractarian movements, while the government relaxed and then finally removed the restrictive penal laws against Catholics throughout the British Isles.

The history ends with the reestablishment of the Roman Catholic hierarchy, with new dioceses and cathedrals in England— what John Henry Newman called "the Second Spring"—and conversions and a great literary revival that boasted authors like G. K. Chesterton, Gerard Manley Hopkins, Ronald Knox, and many others (chapters 9 and 10).

Throughout the text there are short biographies of great martyrs, artists, poets, and converts. Their stories enliven the history of the English Reformation and exemplify the drama of the various stages of this history.

I based this book on a class I taught at the Spiritual Life Center of the Catholic Diocese of Wichita, Kansas, in June 2005. The students and the director of adult education encouraged me to turn my classes into a book. The result is a story of the English Reformation that also tells how Catholics dealt with discrimination, mistrust, lack of religious freedom, and treatment as second-class citizens up to the mid-nineteenth century. Since it is an introduction, the suggested reading list at the end is essential for gaining deeper understanding of certain people and topics.

Because there are many important characters named Mary, Anne, Catherine, James, Charles, and Henry, I have provided a family tree for the Tudor and the Stuart families, and list of important historical figures. I have also prepared a list of important theological and political terms and a timeline of historic events.

Family Trees

THE HOUSE OF TUDOR

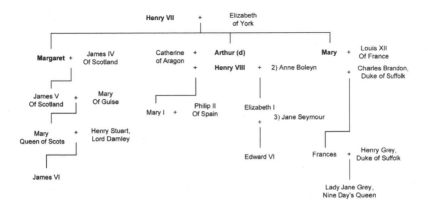

Henry VII + Elizabeth of York

Margaret + James IV Of Scotland

Catherine of Aragon + Arthur (d)
+ Henry VIII + 2) Anne Boleyn

Mary + Louis XII Of France
+ Charles Brandon, Duke of Suffolk

James V Of Scotland + Mary Of Guise

Mary I + Philip II Of Spain

Elizabeth I
3) Jane Seymour

Mary Queen of Scots + Henry Stuart, Lord Darnley

Edward VI

Frances + Henry Grey, Duke of Suffolk

James VI

Lady Jane Grey, Nine Day's Queen

THE HOUSE OF STUART

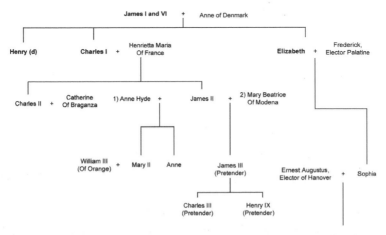

James I and VI + Anne of Denmark

Henry (d)

Charles I + Henrietta Maria Of France

Elizabeth + Frederick, Elector Palatine

Charles II + Catherine Of Braganza

1) Anne Hyde + James II + 2) Mary Beatrice Of Modena

William III (Of Orange) + Mary II   Anne

James III (Pretender)

Ernest Augustus, Elector of Hanover + Sophia

Charles III (Pretender)   Henry IX (Pretender)

George I

Important Historical Figures

THE TUDOR ERA

Kings and Queens

1. **Henry VII**—Founder of the Tudor dynasty; defeated Richard III at Bosworth Field; married Elizabeth of York, uniting the Houses of Lancaster and York and ending the Wars of the Roses. Four surviving children: Arthur, Henry, Mary, and Margaret. Daughters Mary and Margaret married to King Louis XII of France and King James IV of Scotland, respectively.

2. **Henry VIII**—Successor to Henry VII after death of older brother Arthur; married Arthur's widow Catherine of Aragon after he became King of England. Renaissance prince and Defender of the Faith who broke away from Rome and established the Church of England under his headship in order to divorce his first wife, Catherine of Aragon, and marry Anne Boleyn.

3. **Catherine of Aragon**—First married to Arthur, then to his brother Henry; daughter of Ferdinand of Aragon and Isabella of Castile, King and Queen of Spain; mother of Mary I.

4. **Anne Boleyn**—Second wife of Henry VIII; mother of Elizabeth I; tried and executed for adultery and incest.

5. **Jane Seymour**—Third wife of Henry VIII; mother of Edward VI; died after childbirth.

6. **Anne of Cleves**—Fourth wife of Henry VIII; marriage annulled; Henry gave her a generous settlement and she remained in England; last of his wives to die.

7. **Catherine Howard**—Fifth wife of Henry VIII; many years his junior; cousin of Anne Boleyn; tried and executed for adultery.

8. **Catherine Parr**—Sixth wife of Henry VIII; good stepmother to Edward, Mary, and Elizabeth; survived Henry by one year.

9. **Edward VI**—Son and heir of Henry VIII; died before he reached adulthood; during his reign as a minor, Protestant Reformation of worship and doctrine spread in England.

10. **Mary I**—Succeeded Edward VI; married Philip II of Spain; led reunion with Rome and restoration of Catholic worship and doctrine during brief reign.

11. **Elizabeth I**—Succeeded Mary I; her long reign saw the Church of England established as the official church; excommunicated by Pope St. Pius V; Catholic recusancy began during her reign.

12. **Lady Jane Grey**—Nine Days Queen, chosen by the Duke of Northumberland to succeed Edward VI; granddaughter of Henry VIII's sister Mary and her second husband Charles Brandon, Duke of Suffolk; executed by Mary I after attempted coup d'état.

13. **Philip II of Spain**—Married Mary I; enemy of Elizabeth I; organized huge Armada to invade England and reestablish Catholicism.

14. **Charles V, Holy Roman Emperor**—Nephew of Catherine of Aragon; protector and advisor to Mary I; resigned as Holy Roman Emperor and retreated to monastery, where he died.

15. **Mary of Scotland**—Granddaughter of Margaret Tudor and James IV of Scotland; her parents were James V and Mary of Guise; she became Queen of Scotland as an infant when her father died; married the Dauphin of France; briefly reigned as Queen of France; returned to Scotland as rival claimant to Elizabeth's throne.

CHURCH AND GOVERNMENT OFFICIALS

1. **Thomas Wolsey, Cardinal Archbishop of York and Lord Chancellor**—Henry VIII's great partner in making England and Henry a power rivaling France and the Holy Roman Empire. Disgraced and dismissed when he failed to achieve papal authorization to annul marriage to Catherine of Aragon. Henry VIII and Anne took over Wolsey's substantial estates and

houses. After living in exile in his own archdiocese, Wolsey died on the way to trial in London.

2. **Thomas More, Chancellor**—Canonized as St. Thomas More, patron saint of lawyers; Renaissance man, friend of Erasmus; succeeded Wolsey as first lay Lord Chancellor but resigned to avoid the issue of Henry VIII's divorce, remarriage, and supremacy of the Church; arrested and tried for treason; beheaded.

3. **John Fisher, Bishop of Rochester**—Later St. John Fisher; reforming bishop and leader of efforts to educate priests well at Cambridge and Oxford; defender of Catherine of Aragon; arrested and tried for treason; named cardinal before being beheaded.

4. **Thomas Cromwell, Lord Chancellor**—Leader of efforts after Wolsey's death to arrange Henry VIII's divorce and remarriage; organized the visitation and dissolution of the monasteries in England; executed after Henry rejected Anne of Cleves as fourth wife.

5. **Thomas Cranmer, Archbishop of Canterbury**—Declared Henry VIII's marriage to Catherine of Aragon null; married Henry and Anne Boleyn; author of the *Book of Common Prayer*; imprisoned under Mary I; first recanted Protestant beliefs and reconciled with the Catholic Church; then recanted and burned at the stake.

6. **Stephen Gardiner, Archbishop of Winchester**—Assisted Henry VIII with organization of Church of England along more conservative Catholic lines; rival to Protestant opponent Cranmer; served as Mary I's Lord Chancellor.

7. **Thomas Howard, Duke of Norfolk**—Uncle of both Anne Boleyn and Catherine Howard, executed queens of England; led response to the Pilgrimage of Grace in reaction to the dissolution of the monasteries; part of Catholic faction at Court near the end of Henry's reign; imprisoned and scheduled for execution when Henry died. His son, Henry Howard, was executed, but Thomas survived.

8. **Thomas Wriothesley, Lord Chancellor**—Another member of the Catholic faction during Henry VIII's last years; tried to

arrest Catherine Parr for heresy. Forced out of power when Henry died and the Seymour family took over.

9. **Edward Seymour, Duke of Somerset**—First Lord Protector of Edward VI; his brother Thomas Seymour married Catherine Parr, Henry VIII's widow, and was executed for attempting a coup d'état; the Duke of Somerset became unpopular and was tried and executed, being replaced by John Dudley.

10. **John Dudley, Duke of Northumberland**—Second Lord Protector of Edward VI; attempted to change the succession to Protestant Lady Jane Grey rather than Catholic Mary I upon Edward VI's death; plot failed; Northumberland was arrested and executed.

11. **Reginald Pole, Cardinal Archbishop of Canterbury**—Childhood friend of Mary I; his mother Margaret Pole was executed because of his efforts in exile against Henry VIII's break from Rome; appointed papal legate and the last Catholic Archbishop of Canterbury during Mary's reign; architect of Catholic restoration; died hours after Mary.

12. **John Knox**—Protestant Reformer; wrote work titled *First Blast of the Trumpet Against the Monstrous Regiment of Women*; not welcomed in Elizabeth I's England, he went to Scotland and led the establishment of the Protestant Presbyterian Kirk of Scotland; Mary, Queen of Scots debated religion with him.

13. **Pope Clement VII**—Pope called upon to decide matter of Henry VIII's divorce from Catherine of Aragon; finally had to excommunicate the former Defender of the Faith when Henry gave himself supremacy over the Church of England.

14. **Pope Julius III**—Pope when Mary I came to the throne; appointed Reginald Pole as papal legate and last Catholic Archbishop of Canterbury.

15. **Pope St. Pius V**—Pope who excommunicated Elizabeth I and declared that her Catholic subjects need not obey her; action led to Catholic recusancy laws.

16. **Pope Gregory XIII**—Pope who assisted Dr. William Allen in establishing secular and Jesuit seminaries for English Catholics in exile.

18. **Dr. William Allen**—Founder of English seminaries in Douai, Rheims, and Rome.

19. **Fr. Edmund Campion**—Later St. Edmund Campion, martyr; bright light of Elizabethan Oxford; studied in Rome in the Jesuit order; returned to England to serve recusant Catholics; arrested, tortured, tried, and executed by drawing, hanging, and quartering.

STUART ERA/HANOVERIAN ERA

Kings and Queens

1. **James I and VI**—Son of Mary Queen of Scots and Henry, Lord Darnley; succeeded Elizabeth I and united the kingdoms of England, Scotland, and Ireland under his rule.

2. **Charles I**—Son of James I and Anne of Bohemia; married Henrietta Maria of France; conflicts with Parliament over finances and religion led to English Civil War; executed by decree of the House of Commons.

3. **Charles II**—Eldest surviving son of Charles I and Henrietta Maria of France; lived in exile with French court; married Catholic princess Catherine of Braganza and had no legitimate children.

4. **James II**—Younger son of Charles I; married first to Anne Hyde, with two daughters, Mary and Anne; converted to Catholicism; married to Mary Beatrice of Modena. His actions to re-establish Catholicism in England and the birth of Catholic Prince of Wales, James Francis, led to his forced abdication when William of Orange invaded at invitation of Parliament; in exile in France he was called the Old Pretender; defeated in his attempt to regain throne at the Battle of the Boyne.

5. **William III and Mary II**—Mary was the eldest daughter of James II and Anne Hyde; she married William of Orange, the great Protestant rival of Louis XIV; William and Mary ruled after James fled England and Parliament declared that he had abdicated.

6. **Anne**—Sister of Mary II; succeeded after death of William III; no surviving children, so the succession passed to the

Protestant House of Hanover, bypassing her Catholic half-brother James Francis.

7. **George I**—Elector of Hanover, succeeded Anne; more interested in events in Germany, he was not popular in England, but ruled through the Whig party, dismissing the Tory party from the administration and convocation, leaving both church and state under the control of the Whigs.

8. **George III**—King of England who lost the American colonies, but who also assisted the Stuart pretenders in exile.

9. **Louis XIV**—The Sun King of France, model for Charles II and refuge for James II.

10. **Louis XV**—King of France who assisted the Stuart pretenders in exile during the attempted invasion of 1745.

STUART PRETENDERS

1. **James III**—The Young Pretender; Son of James II and Mary Beatrice of Modena; birth was clouded by rumors of deception; led the invasion of 1715. Married Clementina Sobieski of Poland; their sons Charles and Henry continued as Stuart Pretenders to the throne.

2. **Charles III**—Known as Bonnie Prince Charlie; led the invasion of 1745; defeated at Culloden; married Princess Louise of Stolberg-Gedern, but had no legitimate children.

3. **Henry IX**—Younger brother of Bonnie Prince Charlie; became priest and then cardinal in Rome; served as camerlengo when Pope Benedict XIV died. Last of the direct descendants and Stuart pretenders.

CHURCH AND GOVERNMENT OFFICIALS

1. **William Laud, Archbishop of Canterbury**—Arminian, High Church Anglican leader of the Church of England under Charles I; tried to force Scotland's Presbyterian Kirk to adopt *Book of Common Prayer*; tried and executed by Parliament.

2. **Oliver Cromwell**—General of the New Model Army of the Parliament during the Civil War; became Lord Protector of England

after the defeat of the royalists and execution of Charles I; succeeded briefly by his son Richard Cromwell, but commonwealth
and protectorate ended with the Restoration of Charles II.

3. **William Sancroft, Archbishop of Canterbury**—Refused to
   read the Declaration of Indulgence as ordered by James II;
   arrested and then acquitted of charges of treason; joined with
   other Tory and Whig leaders to call William of Orange to save
   the Church of England from James II's attempts to reassert
   Catholicism; then refused to swear the oath to William III and
   Mary II, thus becoming one of the first group of non-juring
   bishops to be deprived of their sees.

4. **William Law**—One of the bishops in the Church of England
   who refused to swear the oath of allegiance to George I, as part
   of the second group of non-jurors. Author of several works of
   devotion and spirituality, including *The Call to the Serious and
   Devout Life*.

5. **John Wesley**—Leader of the Methodist Movement, reviving
   the Church of England, with the "method" of sermons, bible
   study, discipline, and charitable works.

6. **Charles Wesley**—John Wesley's brother and fellow Methodist,
   author of classic hymns such as, "Christ the Lord is Risen
   Today" and "Love Divine, All Loves Excelling."

7. **Richard Challoner, Vicar Apostolate**—During the eighteenth
   century, Challoner wrote many works of history, catechesis, and
   devotion to assist Catholics in England at perhaps the lowest
   point of their history.

8. **John Henry Newman**—Former leader of the Oxford Movement in the Church of England; became a Roman Catholic and
   founder of the Oratory in England; great apologist and writer,
   most famous for his *Apologia Pro Vita Sua*, defending his conversion. Pope Leo XIII named him a cardinal.

9. **Henry Edward Manning, Archbishop of Westminster**—One
   of the many converts who followed Newman into the Roman
   Catholic Church; he became the second Archbishop of Westminster after the restoration of the hierarchy in England and
   was named a cardinal.

Important Theological and Political Terms

1. **Protestant; Evangelical**—General term for those who rejected the authority of the pope in Rome or some other central Catholic doctrine such as the sacraments.

2. **Lutherans**—Followers of Martin Luther, who started the Reformation in Germany. Luther's theology included justification by faith alone and some form of belief in the Real Presence of the Eucharist.

3. **Calvinists**—Followers of Jean Calvin, French leader of the Reformation in Geneva, Switzerland. Calvinist doctrine is summed up in five points: total depravity; unconditional election; limited atonement; irresistible grace; and perseverance of the saints.

4. **Zwinglians**—Followers of Huldrych Zwingli, leader of the Reformation in Zurich, Switzerland. Zwinglian doctrine was closer to Lutheranism but viewed the Eucharist as more of a symbol of Jesus's presence and not the Real Presence.

5. **Arminianism**—Rejection of Calvinist doctrines regarding grace and free will cooperation with God's grace. Named after the Dutch Theologian Jacobus Arminius, this theology of salvation stressed man's ability and need to respond to grace and the limited depravity of the human condition that made such response possible.

6. **Recusancy**—Refusal to take oaths. Roman Catholics in England refused to take the Oaths of Allegiance and Supremacy from the reign of Elizabeth I until the nineteenth century, when Catholic emancipation removed the statements against the pope and the Real Presence in the Eucharist as described by the term Transubstantiation.

7. **Puritan**—English Calvinist, rejecting Arminian theology. From the reign of Elizabeth I through the commonwealth and protectorate, Puritans wanted greater purification of the Church of England from Catholic influences, including the episcopal structure of bishops and hierarchy.

8. **Anglicanism**—Specific form of English Protestantism, primarily maintaining a sacramental system and hierarchy, but rejecting many Catholic doctrines. Sometimes called the Via Media because it is a way between Roman Catholicism and Calvinism or Lutheranism.

9. **Presbyterianism**—Specific form of Calvinism developed by John Knox in Scotland, where the church was called the Kirk.

10. **Monastic Orders**—Several orders established monasteries throughout England, which Henry VIII dissolved between 1535–1537. These included the Augustinian Canons, who followed a rule derived from the teaching of St. Augustine of Hippo; the Premonstratensian or Norbertine White Canon; and the Carthusians, also called the Order of St. Bruno, who lived in charterhouses which combined eremitical (hermit) and cenobitic (community) life. The Cluniac and Cistercian orders, following the rule of St. Benedict of Nursia, also founded famous abbeys.

11. **Counter-Reformation**—Efforts by the Roman Catholic Church to respond to the Reformations of Luther, Calvin, Zwingli, and others by clarifying Church teaching, reforming clerical education and behavior, rebuilding churches, and apologetic works to defend Church teaching. The Council of Trent met from 1545 to 1563 to develop the founding documents of the Counter-Reformation.

12. **Erastianism**—Taken from the name of Thomas Erastus, Erastianism holds that the church should be subordinated to the state and that the state should control the church, even in matters of discipline and administration.

13. **Latitudinarianism**—Belief that within the Church matters of doctrine, worship, and hierarchy are much less important than behavior or moral development.

14. **The Enlightenment**—Philosophical movement in Europe in the eighteenth century led by writers and thinkers such as Voltaire, David Hume, John Locke, and others. Enlightenment thinkers primarily emphasized the superiority of reason over faith; skepticism over belief; freedom over obedience.

15. **Tory party**—Political party that developed during the reign of Charles II, dedicated to protecting the legitimate succession, the position of the Church of England, and the rule of the monarch. The opposing party (see Whig) named them the Tories, which has a derogatory sense meaning "Papist Irish Thugs." The Tory party in politics allied with the high church party in the Church of England. It is the antecedent of today's Conservative party in England.

16. **Whig party**—Political party that developed during the reign of Charles II, dedicated to excluding the legitimate (Catholic) heir, James II, in favor of the illegitimate (Protestant) heir, James Monmouth. They also emphasized the power and authority of Parliament over the king's authority. The opposing party (see Tory) called these exclusionists the Whigs, which has a derogatory sense meaning "covenanting Scottish cattle thieves." The term Whig also applies to the theory of English history developed by Thomas Macaulay and George Trevelyan, emphasizing the progressive course of liberalism in England as something inevitable and good. The Whig party is the antecedent of today's Labour party in England.

410 Years of Historic Events

Date	Event
1485	Battle of Bosworth Field; Richard III defeated; Henry Tudor (Henry VII), succeeds as King of England, founding the Tudor Dynasty
1501	Marriage of Arthur, Prince of Wales, to Catherine of Aragon; Death of Arthur; Catherine remains in England, pending remarriage
1509	Death of Henry VII; accession of Henry VIII, who marries Catherine
1515	Thomas Wolsey, Archbishop of York, becomes Henry's chancellor; Henry and Wolsey contend with Charles V, Holy Roman Emperor, and Francois I of France for leadership of Europe
1516	Birth of Mary, only surviving child of Henry VIII and Catherine of Aragon
1521–1522	Henry begins to investigate feasibility of divorce/annulment; Anne Boleyn comes to court
1529	Papal legate comes to England for hearing on the validity of the marriage; Catherine defended by John Fisher, Bishop of Rochester—no decision reached
1529	Fall of Wolsey; Thomas More succeeds him as chancellor
1531	Catherine and Mary removed from court and separated

1533	Death of William Warham, Archbishop of Canterbury; Thomas Cranmer succeeds him: declares Henry's marriage to Catherine null; officiates at wedding of Henry and Anne; Anne crowned queen
1533–1535	Separation from Catholic Church; Henry named Supreme Head and Governor of the Church of England by convocation of bishops and Parliament
1533	Birth of Elizabeth, only surviving child of Henry and Anne
1535	Arrest, trial, and execution of Thomas More and John Fisher; Thomas Cromwell succeeds More as chancellor
1535–1536	Death of Catherine of Aragon; arrest, trial, and execution of Anne Boleyn; Mary declared heir once more; Elizabeth declared illegitimate; Henry marries Jane Seymour one month after Anne's execution
1535–1537	Cromwell coordinates visitation and dissolution of monasteries; reaction of the Pilgrimage of Grace in northern England
1537	Birth of Edward; death of Jane. Henry establishes the succession: Edward, Mary, Elizabeth
1540	Henry marries Anne of Cleves; immediately divorces her. Fall and execution of Cromwell; Thomas Wriothesley succeeds as chancellor
1540–1542	Henry marries Catherine Howard; execution of Catherine Howard for adultery
1543	Henry marries Catherine Parr
1547	Death of Henry VIII; accession of Edward VI, minority king with Edward Seymour as protector
1548	Thomas Cranmer issues the *Book of Common Prayer*; Parliament suppresses the Catholic Mass; prayer book revolts in western England

1549–1550	Edward Seymour executed; John Dudley, Duke of Northumberland succeeds as protector
1552–1553	Edward VI's illness; Northumberland's attempt to change the succession; death of Edward; temporary accession of Jane Grey; Mary thwarts the coup.
1553	Mary crowned Queen of England; return of the Catholic Mass; relationship with Rome reestablished; Parliament rescinds Edward's Reformation legislation
1554	Reginald Pole returns from exile as papal legate and Archbishop of Canterbury, last Catholic in that office
1554	Wyatt's Rebellion; execution of Lady Jane Grey
1554	Mary weds Philip of Spain, King of Naples and son of Charles V
1555–1558	Revival of heresy laws; executions at Smithfield
1558	Death of Mary, last Catholic Queen of England; accession of Elizabeth
1559–1563	Acts of Settlement and Uniformity passed by Parliament; Catholic bishops refused oath of allegiance, replaced by Protestant bishops
1560	Return of Mary Stuart from France as Queen of Scotland; beginning of plots and plans to remove Elizabeth and replace her with Mary
1568–1569	Catholic revolts in northern England; defeated
1568	Fall of Mary, Queen of Scots; exiled in England and prisoner of Elizabeth
1570	Pope St. Pius V excommunicates Elizabeth; beginning of recusant era
1580	Edmund Campion, first of many Jesuits and other priests, returns to England to minister to Catholics
1581	Martyrdom of Edmund Campion

1582	Catholic Europe adopts Gregorian calendar; England maintains the Julian calendar
1584–1585	Elizabeth supports the Protestants in the Spanish Netherlands against Spanish Catholic rule
1587	Execution of Mary, Queen of Scots
1588	Defeat of Spanish Armada
1594–1597	Richard Hooker writes *The Laws of Ecclesiastical Polity*, theological explanation of Anglican Via Media
1594–1603	War with Irish lords
1603	Defeat of Irish lords; death of Elizabeth; accession of James VI of Scotland, son of Mary, Queen of Scots, as James I of England
1605	The Gunpowder Plot discovered; additional recusancy laws against Catholics
1611	The authorized "King James" version of the Holy Bible
1625	Death of James I; accession of Charles I, married to Henrietta Maria, sister of King Louis XIII of France
1626–1633	Charles in conflict with Parliament over religion, foreign policies, and funding
1629–1632	George Calvert, First Lord Baltimore, works to establish colony in Maryland, which will not have an established church, allowing freedom of religious practice
1632–1675	Cecil Calvert, Second Lord Baltimore, becomes proprietor and governor of Maryland colony
1633–1640	Personal rule (without Parliament)
1637	Charles and William Laud, Archbishop of Canterbury, try to force *Book of Common Prayer* on Presbyterians in Scotland

1640–1642	Conflicts between Charles and Puritans in Scotland and England and between Catholics and Protestants in Ireland
1640–1660	Charles forced to recall Parliament for funds— the Long Parliament
1641	The Root and Branch reforming Parliament
1642	Charles raises his standard against Parliament in Oxford
1642–1646	Civil War; rise of Oliver Cromwell as military and political leader
1647	Charles captured; escapes; Second Civil War
1648–1649	Charles captured again, tried, and executed
1649	Maryland Toleration Act mandating religious tolerance
1649	Parliament of Scotland proclaims Charles II King of Scotland
1649–1653	Parliamentary Commonwealth Rule in England: the Rump Parliament
1649–1651	Oliver Cromwell puts down rebellions in Ireland and Scotland
1653–1658	Oliver Cromwell dissolves the Rump Parliament; rules as Lord Protector
1658–1660	Death of Oliver Cromwell; brief accession of his son, Richard
1660	Restoration of the monarchy and the Church of England; Charles II returns to England with the Duke of York as his heir
1661–1679	Cavalier Parliament enacts Clarendon Code to punish Puritans and reestablish Church of England

1668–1669	Conversion of James, the Duke of York, and his wife, Anne Hyde; Charles requires that their daughters Mary and Anne be raised Protestant
1671	The death of Anne Hyde
1672	Charles II attempts to introduce Declaration of Indulgence for Catholics and Protestant dissenters from Church of England
1673	James marries Mary Beatrice of Modena
1675–1688	Charles Calvert, Third Lord Baltimore, becomes proprietor and governor of Maryland colony, losing control upon the Glorious Revolution
1677	Marriage of Mary, the Duke of York's eldest daughter by Anne Hyde, to William of Orange
1678–1682	The Popish Plot and Exclusionist Crisis: wave of Anti-Catholic hysteria, trials, and executions
1681	Titus Oates, fomenter of the Popish Plot, found guilty of sedition
1685	Deathbed conversion of Charles II; accession of James II; attempted invasion by James Monmouth, one of Charles' illegitimate sons
1687	Conflict with Church of England over the Declaration of Indulgence
1688	Birth of Catholic Prince of Wales (James Francis Edward), displacing Protestant daughters Mary and Anne from succession
1688	Leaders of Parliament invite William of Orange to England
1688	James and family flee for France; William and Mary reign as joint rulers
1688–1701	Parliament passes new Acts of Settlement and Succession; only Protestant heirs

1689	Parliament passes Act of Toleration, granting religious freedom to Protestant dissenters, not Catholics (or Unitarians)
1690	James II attempts to retake the throne; loses the Battle of Boyne in Ireland
1694	Mary dies; William reigns alone
1702	William dies; Anne's accession
1702–1713	Wars of the Spanish Succession (Queen Anne's War): England wins
1707	Act of Union: formation of the United Kingdom
1714	Death of Anne; George, Elector of Hanover, succeeds per the 1701 Act of Settlement
1715	James Francis Edward Stuart (James III or Old Pretender) attempts to retake the throne by invasion; defeated in Scotland
1739	John and Charles Wesley begin the Methodist movement
1745	Bonnie Prince Charlie (Charles III or Young Pretender), attempts to retake the throne by invasion; defeated in Scotland; last invasion effort of Stuart pretenders
1752	England finally adopts the Gregorian calendar
1778	First Catholic Relief Act; passage provokes the Gordon Riots
1789–1795	French Revolution: Catholic priests and nuns in exile from the Terror create sympathy in England
1791	Roman Catholic Relief Act; George III rejected full Catholic Emancipation
1800	Act of Union: incorporating Ireland (now Northern Ireland) into United Kingdom

1807	Death of Henry Cardinal Stuart, last direct Stuart pretender
1823–1829	Daniel O'Connell campaigns in Ireland for Catholic emancipation
1829	Parliament passes Catholic Emancipation Act; The Oxford Movement, revival of Church of England authority, liturgy, and significance
1845	John Henry Newman, leader of the Oxford Movement, becomes Catholic (effectively ending the Oxford Movement)
1845–1849	Potato Famine in Ireland; massive emigration of Irish Catholics to America and England
1850	Catholic hierarchy reestablished in England; Nicholas Wiseman the first Archbishop of Westminster
1865–1866	Newman's controversy with Charles Kingsley; writes and publishes *Apologia Pro Vita Sua*
1895	Construction begins on Westminster Cathedral in London

1
PART

THE TUDOR REFORMATIONS

CHAPTER

The Roman Catholic Church in England before the Break from Rome

ENGLISH PARISHES AND MONASTERIES

THE ROMAN CATHOLIC CHURCH in England was strong before Henry VIII broke away from Rome and proclaimed himself the Head and Supreme Governor of the Church of England. There was no Johann Tetzel creating a scandal with the sale of indulgences, and Catholics in England were active in their faith. Catholicism was the source of a culture and way of life, from the womb to the tomb, and even beyond time to eternity. The Church had experienced division and heresy in the previous centuries. Two Plantagenet kings had conflicts with Archbishops of Canterbury and the Pope in Rome. This context is important background to the events in the sixteenth century.

Before the Henrican Reformation, John Wyclif and his Lollard followers in the latter part of the fourteenth and first half of the fifteenth centuries had protested against some teachings and some abuses in the Church. Lollardy sprang from the Manichean heresies in Southern France. It also reacted against the disorders caused by the Black Death, the Hundred Years War, and the "Babylonian Captivity," when the popes left Rome and lived in the south of France. The Lollard movement was anti-clerical, and is sometimes seen as a precursor of the Reformation in England. Wyclif, an

Oxford theologian, and his followers taught that it was necessary that the priest be in the state of grace for the sacraments to be effective—a revival of the early Donatist heresy that St. Augustine battled—and they soon came to regard the Holy Bible as the sole source of religious faith.

The government of England responded to the Lollards with anti-heresy laws during the reigns of the later Plantagenet kings, but Lollards, in smaller numbers, were tried and executed under both Henry VII and Henry VIII. The Church responded, as W. A. Pantin argues in his study of the Church in the fourteenth century, with efforts to reform the moral behavior, education and formation, and placement of priests. Catechetical and spiritual formation of the laity were also important, as Pantin notes in *The English Church in the Fourteenth Century.*

It may be tempting to see the Lollards as antecedents of the Protestant movement in England, but as Eamon Duffy points out in the preface to his book, *The Stripping of the Altars,* the Lollards never represented a new religious practice—their practice was criticism of their priests and fellow parishioners: "For all its biblicism, Lollardy presented itself primarily as a critique of religion rather than an alternative religion, and after 1414 it seems to have displayed an unstoppable tendency to slide into the ideology of the village know all. The hostile [secular] court records" seem to reveal "essentially a family tradition with little apparent evangelical appeal or motivation."[2]

The Lollard movement certainly shows that some Christians felt discontent with the Church. But they were not truly reformers, and much of their appeal had faded by Henry VIII's time—Lollardy did not inspire sixteenth-century Protestantism in England.

Another pattern in English history that seems to anticipate the English Reformation was the series of disputes between English kings and the pope. Henry II fought with Thomas à Becket in the twelfth century over the right of clergy to appeal to Roman clerical courts, instead of undergoing trial in English secular courts. Henry's arguably rhetorical question, "Who will rid me of this troublesome priest?" led some of his knights to murder the Archbishop of Canterbury in his cathedral in 1170. The outrage evoked by this act throughout England and Europe led to Henry doing public penance, Thomas à Becket being canonized, the foundation of the great shrine that Chaucer's pilgrims seek in *The Canterbury Tales*, and Henry's acceptance of the right of priests to appeal to Roman clerical courts.

Henry's son John also opposed Pope Innocent III over papal control in the choice of the Archbishop of Canterbury. John was excommunicated and England placed under interdict, without any sacraments, from 1207 to 1212. Eventually John had to submit to the Pope and accept the original choice for Archbishop, Stephen Langton, who would advise the nobles in their presentation of the Magna Carta for John's signature at Runnymede in 1215.

Relations between church and state were often contentious throughout the Middle Ages, not only in England, but also in Europe overall. But the conflicts were not necessarily precursors to Henry VIII's break from Rome, especially since relations between England and Rome had been relatively harmonious since the early thirteenth century. Henry II's concern about clergy availing themselves of ecclesiastical courts continued to rankle with England's rulers, but it was not a critical issue. England and Rome were at peace until the reign of Henry VIII.

At the time Henry VIII's great matter of obtaining a divorce from his first wife arose, Oxford University was solidly Roman Catholic. There had been a strong Lollard presence there during Wyclif's day, but since then Oxford had been orthodox. At Cambridge University, there was a group of scholars who had traveled on the continent and become attracted to Martin Luther's ideas. One of these was Thomas Cranmer, ordained a Catholic priest and also secretly married. His connections to the Continental reformers would influence his writing of the *Book of Common Prayer* during the reign of Edward VI. Under Henry VIII, as we shall see, he was mostly held in check by the Supreme Head and Governor of the Church of England, even keeping his marriage secret because his master did not approve of married priests.

In spite of a history of conflicts with the pope, Lollard dissidents, and a small community of Lutheran followers, the Catholic Church in England was not poised for a Protestant Reformation in the sixteenth century. Instead, as Eamon Duffy has demonstrated with his painstaking research of parish documents in *The Stripping of the Altars*, the lay people of England were well served by the Church. They entered energetically into the liturgical and sanctoral year of fasting, feasting, processing, and observing the seasons of Advent and Christmas, Lent, and Easter. Commemorating and praying for their beloved dead, English men and women contributed to their parishes to provide for the poor, for the celebration of Mass and the sacraments, and to maintain the structure and furnishing of their churches. The communion of saints extended the community of the Church beyond the living to include the faithful departed. The faithful departed included the saints in heaven as intercessors with God for healing, success, holiness, good harvests, and peace. The poor souls in purgatory needed the prayers of the living to join the saints in heaven. Heaven was the goal of the living, as they sought to be free from sin on earth and to do penance for their sins.

In personal devotion and liturgical worship, as Duffy recounts throughout his seminal work, the English were devoted and devout Catholics, in a society that celebrated sacramentally, delighting in the goodness of creation, enjoying the blessings of the harvest, commemorating the seasons and rhythms of life and death. As Susan Brigden comments, "Christian rites and sacrament were central to people's lives. They created and validated relationships, made new affinities, and sanctioned the passage from one stage of life to another."[3]

Both the rich and the poor, the highborn and the low, were involved in the festivities of what we think of as "Merry Old England," as Ronald Hutton describes in his book, *The Rise and Fall of Merry England: The Ritual Year, 1400–1700.* The festivities of the Christmas season, in particular, had a wonderful sense of the world turned upside down, giving the servant the chance to be the master and the master the opportunity to see what a servant experienced. Feasting, festivity, and hospitality were essential to the celebration of Jesus Christ's birth, including carols, the Yule Log, wassail, and other libations. In the Cathedral communities, a choirboy was elected "Bishop" for a day, with a youth fulfilling a hierarchical role with humor and wit. We usually think of the social structure of the Middle Ages as being absolutely rigid. These festive role changes turn that image upside down.

The festivities of the church year and of the seasons of planting and harvest demonstrated community and fellowship. They also had a practical purpose, as ales and fairs raised money for church furnishings and supplies.

The ritual year inspired the drama of the era, as the history of the Mystery plays demonstrates. Written between 1375 and 1450, four cycles of these plays were performed by the Guilds of York, Chester, Wakefield, and near Coventry. They conveyed the truths of salvation from the Fall of Lucifer, through Creation and the Fall of Man, Noah and the Flood, Abraham and Isaac, to the Nativity, Baptism, and Temptation of Jesus, and culminating with the Passion and Resurrection and Doomsday, when Christ returned in glory. Performed around the feast of Corpus Christi, they celebrated the Eucharist, by showing how Jesus Christ and his Church had fulfilled God's promises. Like much of the celebration of the liturgical year in English society, the plays would be suppressed as the Reformation progressed—not with the peoples' approval but with their compliance.

In their personal devotion, Duffy demonstrates, many literate Catholic laity in union with the clergy used prayer books based on the Liturgy of Hours as it was prayed in monasteries and chantries throughout England. In *The English Church in the Fourteenth Century*, W. A. Pantin describes "one of the most important phenomena of the religious history of the later Middle Ages, namely the rise of the devout layman." He notes

> Of course there had been devout laymen in every age, but in the fourteenth and fifteenth centuries it was possible for a devout and literate layman, with the help of all the apparatus of religious instruction, sermons, and devotional literature, to take a more intelligent, educated, active, and, so to speak, professional part in the life of the Church. . . . And of course the institution of the third orders of the mendicants had for a long time past offered lay men and women active membership of and participation in a religious order. To this type of the devout layman, at a later period, belonged such different personalities as King Henry VI and St. Thomas More.[4]

Pantin also stresses that the Church taught parents how to raise their children piously and prayerfully—personal lay piety was not an invention of the Protestant Reformation. The printing press provided mass-market prayer books, sermons, catechisms, and guides for heads of households, instructing fathers on how to teach their children the Apostles' Creed, the Our Father, and the Hail Mary in English.

We should also remember that English Catholics possessed the tremendous works of fourteenth-century mystics: Richard Rolle, Walter Hilton, Julian of Norwich, and the author of *The Cloud of Unknowing*. As Pantin notes, one of the main themes of these works is their "very strong, intimate, and affectionate concentration on and devotion to the Person of Christ" in "a very vivid and even emotional form . . . particularly concentrated on the Passion of Christ and on the Holy Name of Jesus." Since the mystics wrote in the vernacular, their works, like Rolle's *The Form of Perfect Living*, Julian's *Showings*, Hilton's *The Ladder of Perfection*, and the anonymous monk's *The Book of Privy Counseling*, influenced Catholic laymen in the development of a deeper spirituality and love of Jesus.[5]

The laity were also devoted to the great saints of England, traveling on pilgrimage to Canterbury "the holy, blissful martyr for to see" (St. Thomas à Becket), to Walsingham for Our Lady, and, further afield, to St. James Compostella in Spain, to the Holy Land, and to Rome. As Pantin notes, the laity were ready to be both active and contemplative, to do their work in the world and be detached from the world, like Margery Kempe or St. Thomas More. These laymen and laywomen were both devout and literate, and they presented the Church with an opportunity and a challenge. The mystical literature of the late Middle Ages, the devotion and concern for the Church encouraged the laity to be both more contemplative and more active; to seek both their own spiritual perfection and the Church's.[6]

Pantin's thesis is that the Roman Catholic Church in England implemented the reforms of the Lateran Council. They fulfilled the "aims of the thirteenth-century reformers" to produce manuals "to instruct to the parish priest in every detail of his work. . . . [to] use the confessional and pulpit as means of religious instruction and spiritual direction."[7] Duffy concurs, recounting how the *Lay Folk's Mass Book* offered an explanation, in English, of every action of the Mass—how the priest's gestures were related to incidents of Jesus Christ's life and Passion. The inward-focused devotion of the laity at Mass "did, in fact, encompass the essentials of Christian prayer—praise and self-surrender to God, confession of sins, intercession for one's own needs and those of one's 'even-christians', and for the building of community in charity. All of these were focused on the event which made all of them possible and meaningful, the consecration which renewed and gave access to the salvation of mankind on Calvary."[8] Throughout the fifteenth and sixteenth centuries, these devotional books and manuals of instruction provided guidance to both priests and laity in performing their religious duties and deepening their personal devotion to Almighty God, just as the artwork in the cathedrals, churches, and chapels provided instruction on the life of Christ and His saints.

The monasteries, which Henry VIII would eventually dissolve, were an integrated part of English life. There were 825 religious houses in England before the Reformation (502 monasteries, 136 convents, and 187 friaries), with approximately 9,300 religious persons in a total population of 3.5 million, or about one religious person in every 375. The monasteries were often sites of pilgrimage, and their cathedrals, like Canterbury or Winchester, held the relics of great saints, like St. Thomas à Becket or St. Swithin. These religious houses served as centers of prayer, oases of hospitality, givers of charity, and as places set aside for the adoration of God.

In England, Ireland, and Wales the monasteries throughout the centuries had fulfilled several other very practical roles, as Thomas E. Woods, Jr. delineates in *How the Catholic Church Built Western Civilization*. In addition to their familiar role as copiers and savers of classic works of Latin and Greek authors and as creators of magnificent Bible manuscripts, the monks undertook hard manual labor of various kinds. They drained swamps, cleared land, founded their monastic houses and tremendous cathedrals. They developed and introduced agricultural, horticultural, animal husbandry, and technological advances, and they harnessed the power of water to mill, grind, and forge.

During the Tudor era the Benedictine Abbot of Saint Albans, Richard of Wallingford, designed a complex astronomical clock, which made possible the precise celebration of Easter as well as the celebration of Daily Offices. At some point during the coming dissolution, the clock would be lost, but the plans survived.[9] The dissolution of the monasteries would be one of the greatest assaults on Catholic life and religion in England, and would provoke an uprising in the north of England, the Pilgrimage of Grace, that would seriously threaten Henry's authority in 1536. Before his break from Rome, however, the monasteries, like the parishes and the cathedrals throughout England, were a strong part of everyday life in the sixteenth century.

DEFENDER OF THE FAITH: ENGLISH RESPONSE TO THE CONTINENTAL REFORMATIONS

As in any era, on the eve of the Reformation the Church in England needed to address certain abuses. Two leaders of this reform and revival from within the Church would also be victims of Henry's acts of supremacy: Thomas More and John Fisher. As two of the Church's most ardent defenders against Lutheran and Zwinglian attacks, they combined love and concern for the Church, defended her against enemies without, and healed her of errors within.

St. Thomas More (1478–1535) is widely familiar because of the play and movie, "A Man for All Seasons" by Robert Bolt. More was a member of the middle class in England, a lawyer and humanist, author of *Utopia*, and friend of Erasmus and John Colet. More matched a successful, active life in the world with an intense spiritual life of prayer, devotion, and fasting. Before his first marriage, he had considered a Carthusian monastic vocation, and that contemplative spirit remained part of his secular life. A lawyer, scholar, husband, father, friend, public official, and humanist, he practiced self-denial and discipline as diligently as he addressed legal issues and the New Learning.

John Fisher (c.1469–1535), Bishop of Rochester, was also a very holy man, practicing poverty and living a life of prayer while actively leading his diocese. With Henry VIII's grandmother, Margaret

Beaufort, as patron, he supervised at Cambridge University the foundation of St. John's and Christ's Colleges, dedicated to the intellectual preparation of priests. He also served in her professorship of divinity at Cambridge, and helped her found a similar chair at Oxford, all while serving as Chancellor at Cambridge—he even invited the great scholar Erasmus to teach there. He preached the funeral oration for both Margaret Beaufort and Henry VII, indicating his reputation as a preacher and his relationship to the family. As the Bishop of Rochester, he was recognized for his holiness, simplicity of lifestyle, learning and wisdom, and for his efforts to improve his diocese.

More, Fisher, and others like John Colet, the Dean of St. Paul's in London, were dedicated to education for both the laity and the clergy. They sought to improve theological knowledge and aimed to include women, especially of higher rank, in this educational program. They emphasized moral probity and participation in the sacraments and personal devotions, although they sometimes were skeptical of all the pilgrimages and other aspects of late medieval piety.

John Colet was particularly critical of Scholastic theology and philosophy, as they had devolved from the works of St. Thomas Aquinas. He founded the School at St. Paul's in London to foster his vision of education according to the New Learning. A close associate of Erasmus, he shared with the author of *The Praise of Folly* great disdain for any abuse of power by the religious hierarchy. Colet died in September, 1519 just as Martin Luther's Reformation career was beginning to have an influence on the Continent and in England.

At the same time they sought renewal in the Church, Thomas More and Bishop Fisher responded to the Continental Reformation by publishing apologetic and argumentative works. Appealing to the Fathers of the Church, they offered refutations of Lutheran teachings on the Church, the sacraments, the Scriptures, salvation, and many other topics. More engaged William Tyndale in a series of pamphlet debates, defending Catholic doctrine and devotion. In his book, *The King's Good Servant But God's First: The Life and Writings of St. Thomas More*, James Monti demonstrates More's encyclopedic and challenging response to Tyndale and other reformers, on topics ranging from papal authority to Marian devotion, from prayers for the dead to the effectiveness of the sacraments.

Like More, Fisher wrote various works to defend Catholic teaching, including *A Defense of the Priesthood*. He also delivered and published devotional sermons like *The Exposition of the Seven Penitential Psalms* to demonstrate and uphold Catholic devotions and spirituality.

Ironically, this English response to Lutheran errors began with Henry VIII's *Defense of the Seven Sacraments* (*Assertio Septem Sacramentorum*) in 1521. Henry wrote to Pope Leo X that "we believe that no duty is more incumbent on a Catholic sovereign than to preserve and increase the Christian faith and religion and the proofs thereof, and to transmit them preserved thus inviolate to posterity." For this achievement, Henry was honored by the Pope and named Defender of the Faith, having promised the Holy Father that "we shall ever defend and uphold, not only by force of arms but by the resources of our intelligence and our services as a Christian, the Holy Roman Church."[10] Even today, the Monarch of Great Britain retains the title of Defender of the Faith.

Sadly, by 1534 Henry would separate himself and his kingdom from the Holy Roman Catholic Church, setting himself up as the Supreme Head of the Church of England. Pope Clement VII would excommunicate the erstwhile Defender of the Faith in 1535. The story of majestic will and religious change in England begins with Henry VIII's desire for a new wife and a male heir, as we shall see in the next chapter.

CHAPTER

Henry VIII (1509 to 1547) and the Break from Rome

A FAMILY: HENRY, CATHERINE, AND MARY—
AND ANNE BOLEYN, 1521 TO 1535

THE STORY OF THE ENGLISH REFORMATION begins with a family. As the Reformation in England divided many families, it broke this one completely.

The Tudor family came to the throne when Henry VII became king in 1485, defeating Richard III at Bosworth Field and ending the Wars of the Roses, the dynastic conflict between the houses of Lancaster and York. To establish his family, he arranged marriages for his children with other ruling families of Europe. His eldest daughter, Margaret, married the King of Scotland, while Mary, the younger daughter, married the King of France. The Prince of Wales, Arthur, married Catherine of Aragon, daughter of King Ferdinand and Queen Isabella of Spain. Henry had not even received Catherine's entire dowry when Arthur died. His second son, also named Henry, became Prince of Wales and heir, and Henry VII petitioned the Pope for the necessary dispensation for the Prince to marry his brother's widow. One of the grounds for seeking the dispensation was that Arthur and Catherine had not consummated their marriage and she was still a virgin. After Henry VII died in 1509, Henry VIII married Catherine and she became his Queen.

They were a popular ruling couple. He was handsome and athletic, and she was pious and charitable. Catherine was an able ruler herself, serving as Regent for Henry when he was away on foreign wars. In 1513, under her Regency the English defeated the Scots army at the Battle of Flodden, while Henry won the Battle of Spurs and conquered Tournai (now in Belgium) in France. Flodden was a much greater victory than Tournai, but Catherine humbly offered it to Henry as the sovereign and ruler. She was a loyal and long-suffering wife, enduring his infidelities and several pregnancies that ended either in miscarriage or stillbirth. The only surviving child was Mary, born in 1516 and heir to the throne.

Henry was very concerned about leaving a female heir. Unlike France, England did not have any Salic laws forbidding a female monarch, but the brief reign of England's only previous queen, Matilda, had been fraught with civil war and rebellion, as the nobles could not accept a female as ruler. The memory of that disastrous reign troubled Henry, who feared similar disruptions. Henry did consider having his illegitimate son named his legal heir and negotiated several marriages of state for Mary. But neither solution in his view provided England with enough stability.

The appearance at court of Anne Boleyn around 1521 or 1522 exacerbated Henry's concerns about his marriage. He had begun to think that God had not blessed his marriage with a son because he had sinned by marrying his brother's widow. Anne Boleyn was the sister of one of Henry's former mistresses (named Mary), but Anne refused to be like her sister and demanded that she become Henry's wife—and Queen.

Anne Boleyn brought to Henry's attention William Tyndale's book, *On the Obedience of Christian Man and How Christian Rulers Ought to Govern*. Tyndale's message that the king, and not the pope, *should* be supreme ruler in his country on matters of both church and state, spoke directly to Henry's predicament. Here was a rationale for what Henry sought—supreme mastery so he could achieve his will: an honorable end of his first marriage; Anne Boleyn as his wife and queen; and a healthy, legitimate son as his heir. According to Tyndale (with whom Thomas More had debated on the sacraments and the Church) Henry should take over the role of the pope in England. It is important to note, however, that Tyndale would not have supported Henry's divorce and remarriage to Anne. In that regard Tyndale was not Anne's ally. In fact, Tyndale's public condemnation of Henry's divorce and remarriage briefly united Henry and Charles V, as Henry asked Charles to arrest Tyndale and return him to England to face Henry's wrath. Henry was also opposed to Tyndale's unauthorized translation of Holy Scripture into English, with notes and introductions that definitely opposed Catholic doctrine. Tyndale was executed for heresy in Vilvoorde, Belgium in 1536, a year after Thomas More and John Fisher were executed at the Tower of London.

In the meantime, Henry and his Chancellor, Thomas Wolsey, the Cardinal Archbishop of York, started the process of gathering evidence that Henry and Catherine's marriage should be dissolved. They consulted with the Convocation of Bishops and with the faculties at Oxford and Cambridge, and began to petition the Vatican for an annulment. Henry also had to petition Rome for a dispensation to marry Anne after having had a prior physical relationship with her sister. Thus, Henry asked the Pope to dissolve one marriage on the grounds of Catherine's prior relationship with Arthur, while he asked for permission to marry Anne in spite of his prior relationship with Mary.

Pope Clement VII would not grant Henry's requests. The Pope was under attack by Charles V, the Holy Roman Emperor, whose armies sacked and destroyed Rome. Charles V was Catherine of Aragon's nephew, and Henry had always been concerned about the diplomatic and political repercussions of his efforts. Catherine of Aragon absolutely refused to cooperate; it had been suggested that she retreat to a convent and allow Henry to marry again, but her concern for Mary and her sense of justice prevented any such compromise. Wolsey's last effort was to bring a papal legatine court to England to try the case of the King's marriage. When Catherine appeared in the court, she spoke only to Henry, asking him how she had offended him; reminding him that she had been a virgin when they were first married—and that he knew the truth—and of all the children she had borne for him. She told him that she would not respond to this court. To her, there was no issue to be tried: they were man and wife, legally, morally, sacramentally, and truly. Then she left the court. She would not return, and the court could not render a decision. Not even Shakespeare in his play *Henry VIII* could improve on the drama and impact of Catherine's appearance in court.

Because Wolsey failed, Anne persuaded Henry to banish the Chancellor to his diocese in York—where he finally became an active bishop, and a very effective one, too. Henry confiscated Wolsey's great palace, Hampton Court, which he had coveted when entertained by his chancellor.

Henry selected Thomas More to be his new chancellor. More stayed away from the issue of the divorce, the "King's Great Matter." When Henry finally made his move to split from Rome, take over control of the Church in England, and divorce Catherine of Aragon so as to marry Anne Boleyn, More resigned his position and retired from public life, hoping for obscurity and withdrawal from the issues of supremacy and succession. When Henry's advisors attempted to break through that silence, he was imprisoned in the Tower of London.

Henry ordered that Catherine and Mary be separated and sent away from court; Catherine's title officially became the Queen Dowager and the Princess became the Lady Mary. Thomas Cromwell took over Wolsey's efforts to settle the matter, while Wolsey died on his way from York for trial in 1530, lamenting that he had served the wrong master, leaving him naked and vulnerable to his enemies—his erstwhile master Henry VIII and Anne Boleyn.

THE BREAK FROM ROME, 1535 TO 1536

When the Archbishop of Canterbury William Warham died in 1533, Henry was able to appoint Thomas Cranmer. He abrogated his loyalty oath to the Pope almost immediately and determined that Henry's marriage to Catherine was invalid. By this time, Henry and Anne had married secretly—so the King was briefly a bigamist—and Anne was pregnant.

Henry now moved to make himself the Supreme Head and Governor of the Church in England and to separate that Church from the Holy Roman Church he had sworn to defend in 1521. He had the help of his new Chancellor, Thomas Cromwell, and his Archbishop of Canterbury, Thomas Cranmer, who both wanted the radical reformation of the Church according to Lutheran teaching. Both the Convocation of Bishops (except for John Fisher, Bishop of Rochester) and the Parliament gave Henry the authority to lead the Church, as far as the law of Christ allowed. They hoped that such a phrase would limit Henry's authority in some way. Acts of Parliament—not of the Convocation of Bishops—in 1534 denied the Pope any influence in the naming of Bishops, ended the practice of sending Peter's Pence to Rome, and placed the decisions of the Convocation of Bishops' under the approval of the King. All appeals to Rome for any judgment were illegal; the King would rule on all religious matters in England: Henry would be England's pope. The Convocation of Bishops never agreed to these actions: these were actions and matters of state, and this pattern of the state (king and Parliament) taking over the role of the Convocation will continue— with one exception—throughout the Tudor dynasty.

Along with Henry's break from Rome and marriage to Anne came a change in who would inherit the throne. Acts of Parliament in 1534 declared the marriage of Henry and Catherine null and void, and stipulated that Elizabeth, Henry and Anne's daughter born in 1533, or any other children of their union would succeed to the throne. Mary was declared illegitimate. Everyone was required to accept without question the marriage of Henry and Anne, now crowned his queen.

The first Catholic martyrs of the English Reformation refused to swear the oaths as Henry and Parliament required. Thomas More and John Fisher were held in the Tower of London before their executions. More told his daughter that he saw the Carthusians of the Charterhouse in London going off to their deaths by hanging, drawing, and quartering as cheerfully as bridegrooms to their marriages. The Carthusians were brutally punished. Besides those who were hung, drawn, and quartered, others were left hung to die of exposure and starvation, and others were starved in prison. More knew these men well: he had nearly joined the Carthusians and had often gone to the Charterhouse for retreats.

More withstood the efforts of friends, family, and interrogators to persuade him either to swear the Oath of Allegiance to Henry VIII or directly to oppose the King and break the law. St. John Fisher, unlike Thomas More, publicly opposed from the beginning Henry's efforts to divorce Catherine and declare his Supremacy. He defended and supported Catherine and spoke up against Henry's action in the Convocation of Bishops. Indeed, he compared himself to St. John the Baptist in his defense of holy matrimony.

Before his execution, Pope Paul III had named John Fisher a cardinal. The pope may have thought that Henry would treat Cardinal Fisher with greater respect. But Henry declared that he would not allow the cardinal's hat to come to England, but instead would send the cardinal's head to Rome. Henry was speaking of his grandmother's confessor. After his long imprisonment in the Tower of London, Fisher was very weak, so that onlookers at his execution were horrified to see his emaciated body. He demonstrated peace and dignity at his death on June 22, 1535. Henry had shown him a kind of mercy by commuting the method of execution, from hanging, drawing, and quartering to beheading. Pope Pius XI canonized John Fisher along with Thomas More in 1935, taking the date of Fisher's death as their shared memorial day.

While in prison, St. Thomas More wrote several devotional works, including *The Sadness of Christ* and *A Dialogue Between Comfort Against Tribulation*. Falsely betrayed by Richard Rich—who also tricked St. John Fisher into making a confidential statement— he finally publicly admitted his opposition to Henry's actions. He was found guilty of treason and sentenced to death, and was beheaded on July 6, 1535. More displayed his wit by joking with the executioner about being helped up the scaffold steps and sparing his beard, which had done nothing wrong. His son-in-law, William Roper, who had adopted some Lutheran tendencies, returned to the Church and wrote *The Life of Thomas More*. The execution of Sir Thomas More shocked the humanist community, but Erasmus was even more shocked that he would be willing to die.

Within a few years, Henry started to tire of Anne, who was extremely jealous of attentions paid to any of her ladies-in-waiting (she had once been Catherine of Aragon's lady-in-waiting). After she had two more pregnancies without a male heir, Henry, attracted now to Jane Seymour, had Anne arrested and tried for adultery and incest. She was found guilty and sentenced to death, and Henry arranged to have a French swordsman brought in as executioner. At the same time, Archbishop Cranmer determined that their marriage was invalid. Within a month of Anne's execution, Henry married Jane Seymour, hoping again for a male heir to the throne.

Now, Elizabeth was no longer Princess and heir, but the Lady Elizabeth, while Mary was no longer the Lady Mary, but Princess and heir. Mary had been forced to swear the same oath by Act of Parliament declaring that her parents had never been validly married, that her father was Supreme Head of the Church in England, and that she would never appeal to the pope. Mary felt that she was betraying her mother, who had died in 1536, but Henry knew she was the focus of those who opposed the changes in religious practice that Parliament began to legislate in 1535 and 1536, especially the dissolution of the monasteries.

THE DISSOLUTION OF THE MONASTERIES
AND THE PILGRIMAGE OF GRACE, 1536 TO 1539

Henry needed money. Before the matter of the divorce, when Cardinal Wolsey was Chancellor, he had pursued a very expensive rivalry with Francois I of France and Charles V of the Holy Roman Empire over who was to be the greatest leader in Europe, and had fought several wars on the Continent. According to George Woodward in his book *The Dissolution of the Monasteries*, Henry "swiftly consumed the treasure his father had carefully hoarded and [this] made him heavily dependent upon parliamentary supply." Wolsey having bullied Parliament and the people to the point of rebellion, Cromwell, who became Henry's Chancellor after the death of Thomas More, sought another source of income. As Woodward notes, "The wealth of the monasteries would naturally catch his eye," and it did so as early as 1534. As secretary to Wolsey, Cromwell had participated in the closure of several small monasteries, so he was familiar with the process and the rewards. And, according to Woodward, Cromwell also had another objective in closing the monasteries: "The monasteries were the chief patrons of and gainers from pilgrimages and relics, and an attack on them would speed the suppression of such superstitions."[11]

Cromwell began by commissioning a process of visitation, to ascertain what possessions the monasteries had and to discover abuses. The crown's first targets were the smaller houses, but the larger ones, as determined by income, also were soon in their sights. The Parliament of 1536 passed laws to dissolve the monasteries. Henry's desires, and the opportunity to raise money without taxes, influenced Parliament more than any abuses Cromwell's visitation found. Although some Protestants would argue that the monastic life neither contributed to the Christian community nor assisted the individual monk to salvation, Henry and Cromwell did not present a theological reason for the dissolution, and the great shrines of Canterbury, Walsingham, Winchester, and others also were destroyed. Henry even enjoyed wearing one of the precious stones from St. Thomas à Becket's shrine, set as a ring for his thumb.

Henry and his commissioners did more than just destroy the tomb of St. Thomas—they worked to destroy the memory of St. Thomas himself. They announced that he would be tried for treason against the King and, if he did not appear, would automatically be found guilty. The proclamation was read before his tomb before they destroyed it. When the dead saint did not appear, he was found guilty, declared never to have been a martyr, and his name was stricken from the calendar of the saints.

In the north of England, common citizens rebelled against the closure of the monasteries and the destruction and confiscation of church artifacts. Led by a gentleman, Robert Aske, the crowds began to press various noblemen to join their cause and grew to a force of almost 60,000. Henry sent Thomas Howard, the Duke of Norfolk to quell the rebellion, but did not have an army large enough to engage the Pilgrimage of Grace. Under a banner depicting the five wounds of Christ, the group demanded an end to the dissolution of the monasteries and the desecration of the churches, the removal of heretical (that is, Protestant) bishops and counselors, the return of papal authority and the restoration of the Lady Mary as legitimate heir. For part of the fall of 1536, Henry lost control of the northern part of his kingdom.

Norfolk and Henry regained control only because Robert Aske did not want to plunge the kingdom into civil war and because he and others in the Pilgrimage believed they were dealing with honorable men. They thought they could trust their king to hear their demands and respond to them reasonably. But Norfolk and Henry were not honest in their dealings with the Pilgrimage of Grace. They made promises they had no intention of keeping so that they could catch the pilgrims in violations of their treaty. Norfolk declared martial law and executed the leaders, including Aske, two abbots, and several noblemen. Henry, desiring revenge, ordered Norfolk to increase the number of executions. Although Geoffrey Moorhouse calls the Pilgrimage of Grace "the rebellion that shook Henry's throne," Henry survived the threat.[12]

Cromwell thus was able to continue with the dissolution of the monasteries and to use the profits to pay the costs of waging war with Scotland and France. By 1539, more than 9,000 monks, nuns, and friars had been removed from their religious houses and pensioned off.

The monks did not always go easily, however, as the story of the last Abbot of Glastonbury shows. Richard Whiting and his monks passed the tests of Cromwell's visitation in 1534. The commissioners found everything as it should be: the monks observed the Rule, and Abbot Whiting was praised for his holy way of life. But, Glastonbury was one of the greatest and richest abbeys in all of England, and Henry could not afford to let its treasures elude him. The fact that Abbot Whiting and his monks had taken the Oath of Supremacy was an obstacle for Henry and Cromwell, but one that could be overcome. The Act of Parliament giving Henry authority to suppress the monasteries required them to be "dissolved, suppressed, renounced or relinquished, forfeited or given up or come into the King's highness by attainder or attainder of treason." So if Abbot Whiting would not give up the monastery willingly, as Dwight Longenecker notes, "Cromwell now had to show the Abbot of Glastonbury to be a traitor"—even though the Abbot had sworn the Oath to Henry and Cromwell's own commissioner had praised him.[13]

What followed sounds like something from the annals of a twentieth-century police state—the Gestapo or the Stasi descending upon the innocent, ignoring the claims of justice and law.

Cromwell's commissioners returned to Glastonbury, arrested Abbot Whiting, and sent him to the Tower of London. They searched his lodgings for incriminating evidence and found none. They searched for the treasures of the Abbey—golden chalices and sumptuous vestments—and found them. They took them for the King.

Cromwell then arranged a trial with a compliant jury and accused Abbot Whiting of robbery, although Cromwell was the robber! The Abbot, the sacrist, and the treasurer were all found guilty and condemned to the death of traitors (hanging, drawing, and quartering). Since Abbot Whiting was a peer of the realm, he was entitled to a trial before Parliament, but Cromwell ignored that law; besides, Parliament was not in session and Cromwell and the King could not wait.

On November 15, 1534 Abbot Richard Whiting was dragged on a hurdle up Tor Hill, hung, disemboweled while still alive, quartered, and decapitated. He was 79 years old, and he had done everything that God and the King of England had required of him. Before he died, he might have seen the empty shell of Glastonbury Abbey, where he had been a monk for 33 years and abbot for nine, where he had been a student at the Abbey school, and where lately there had been a thriving, holy place of prayer, hospitality, and charity. Then he died in agony.

Pope Leo XIII beatified Richard Whiting, his sacrist, Roger James, and treasurer, John Thorne (who were executed separately), in 1895.

The plight of the former nuns was perhaps worse than the surviving monks. Occupations open to them either inside or outside the Church were limited. Former monks could become chantry priests or find other clerical employment, and could even teach or pursue some other scholarly vocation. But for the former nuns, pensioned off with only £5 a year in an inflationary economy, struggled to make new lives, some living with their families, some marrying, some going into exile in France to continue living their religious vocations.

During the French Revolution in the eighteenth century, nuns who lived in French convents established for English exiles had to flee to England, reversing the process. The French Revolutionary government dissolved the monasteries as part of its campaign of de-Christianization after the fall of the most Christian King of France.

Roman Catholicism and Benedictine monasticism had come to England together when Pope St. Gregory the Great sent St. Augustine of Canterbury to convert the Angles into angels in 597—almost a thousand years before. The history of English monasticism was redolent with the names of Venerable Bede, Alcuin of York, St. Anselm of Canterbury, St. Aelred of Rievaulx, St. Stephen Harding, and St. Hugh of Lincoln. Now the majestic will of Henry had destroyed its heritage and contributions to English culture. The Benedictine, Cistercian, Augustinian, Carthusian, Premonstratensian, and Cluniac houses became either new nobles' homes or bare, ruined choirs. (A book like *Abbeys and Monasteries*, with text and photography by Derry Brabbs, published by Weidenfield & Nicolson, depicts vestiges of the glory that was lost.)

Among the great losses were the libraries. Hundreds of manuscripts were destroyed. Of all the great polyphonic choir books of the late medieval era, only three remain. The choir book from Eton contains the only music we have by certain composers, and it is not complete.

The crown obtained the lands and the riches of the shrines and altars, melted down the gold to pay for wars, and used the iron roof materials to make cannons.

THOMAS CROMWELL, THOMAS CRANMER, AND HENRY'S REFORMATION

During Henry's time, Thomas Cromwell and Thomas Cranmer wanted to reform Church doctrine and worship according to Lutheran teaching. As his career continued into Edward VI's reign, Cranmer became more aligned with the Zwinglian understanding of the Church and the sacraments. Henry VIII, however, did not favor Lutheran reforms. It is very likely that he never accepted the crucial Protestant doctrine of justification by faith alone. Although he would not allow a shrine like St. Thomas à Becket's to remain as a reminder of another Thomas who had opposed another Henry over the authority of the pope, he did not deny the communion of saints.

He discouraged the use of the word purgatory, yet allowed prayer for the dead.

Henry presented these beliefs to the Convocation of Bishops in 1536. The convocation was divided: some bishops were Catholic while some were Protestant, but all of them were shocked that a king should define Church doctrine. They had not yet understood what they agreed to in giving control of the Church to their sovereign. Henry required them to accept the Ten Articles, which limited the scope of the Reformation in England.

> The Articles were moderate in tone, and generally were not in opposition to the old theology. They approved of Transubstantiation, emphasized the importance and necessity of Baptism, Penance, and the Eucharist without affirming that these were the only three Sacraments, declared that good works were necessary for justification, that prayers might be offered for those who were dead, that the use of the word purgatory was not to be recommended, that reverence should be shown to images and pictures, and that the older ceremonies should be retained.

Three years later, in 1539, Henry again had to use Parliament to set the religious law of the land.

> The decision was embodied in an Act of Parliament entitled "An Act abolishing diversity of Opinions," which having received the royal assent was placed upon the Statute Book (1539). The Articles agreed upon by Convocation and Parliament and published by the king's authority were: (1) that in the Eucharist the substance of the bread and wine is changed into the Body and Blood of Christ; (2) that Communion under both kinds is not necessary for salvation; (3) that clerical celibacy should be observed; (4) that vows of chastity should be observed; (5) that private Masses ought to be retained; and (6) that auricular confession is expedient. Denial of the first article, namely, that regarding Transubstantiation was to be deemed heresy punishable by death at the stake, and denial of the others was felony punishable by forfeiture for the first and by death for the second offense. Priests who had taken to themselves wives were commanded to put them away under threat of punishment for felony, and people who

refused to confess and receive the Eucharist at the usual times, were to be imprisoned or fined for the first offense, and to be judged guilty of felony for the second offense.[14]

Since the head of the Church of England was neither a loyal Roman Catholic nor an ideological Protestant, the English Reformation under Henry VIII was a mixture of Catholic and Protestant worship, doctrine, and practice. Even after he allowed the publication of an authorized translation of the Bible into English, Henry disapproved of individuals reading the Bible privately and interpreting the scriptures on their own.

Because the destruction of the monasteries resulted in the loss of much medieval polyphonic music, Henry needed a court composer to provide music for services at court. Although he remained a practicing Catholic—who was willing to take the oaths to Henry, of course—one man was able to remain in office through all the religious changes that Henry brought about by the break from Rome. Thomas Tallis (c. 1510–1585) composed and performed music in the Chapel Royal for Henry VIII and all his heirs. He first composed Marian anthems for Cardinal Wolsey. Then he wrote English anthems for Archbishop Cranmer and the new *Book of Common Prayer*. For Archbishop Reginald Pole he prepared florid Latin Masses. Tallis composed psalm chant tunes for Archbishop Matthew Parker's psalter of 1567. In the twentieth century Ralph Vaughn Williams based his *Fantasia on a Theme of Thomas Tallis* on one of those chant tunes. Tallis survived and prospered throughout these changes. Mary rewarded his talent with a lease on a manor in Kent, while Elizabeth granted him a patent to print and publish his works.

On October 12, 1537 Henry's goal of having a legitimate son to succeed him was finally achieved. Jane Seymour died in childbirth, but Edward, the Prince of Wales, survived. Henry now arranged the succession: Edward, who was to rule with a council until he reached his majority; then Mary and her descendants, if Edward had no heir; and then Elizabeth and her descendants, if Mary had no heir.

After Jane Seymour's death, Henry soon sought a fourth wife. Many of the Catholic princesses of Europe would not marry him on grounds of religion and his treatment of Catherine of Aragon and Anne Boleyn. One princess quipped that her own neck was too slender—too much a temptation for the executioner—and another that if she had two heads, she would consent.

At the same time, France and the Holy Roman Empire entered into an alliance. Thomas Cromwell encouraged Henry to make an alliance with a German Protestant country by marrying Anne of Cleves. The court painter Hans Holbein traveled to Cleves, one of the Duchies of northern Germany, and portrayed Anne very flatteringly. As soon as Henry met her in England, however, he proclaimed that he "liked her not." She may not have liked Henry's appearance either, as the slender, handsome Renaissance prince had become an obese, limping, imperious king. Almost immediately, he began to negotiate an annulment and a generous settlement for Anne. Henry blamed Cromwell, removed him from office, stripped him of his property, and had him executed. Anne of Cleves remained in England, and never remarried. She was affectionate to his children and survived Henry by ten years. Ironically, Henry's erstwhile Protestant bride converted to Catholicism.

Henry soon fell in love with Catherine Howard, a cousin of Anne Boleyn, and married her in 1540. This marriage was a hopeful sign for the Catholic party at court, led by Stephen Gardiner and Thomas Howard, but Catherine was condemned and beheaded on charges of adultery in 1542. Henry then married Catherine Parr in 1543. A pious and scholarly Protestant who cared for him in his last illness and brought all his children together in a happier household with education and care, she would survive him by only a year, dying in childbirth in 1548.

Henry, upset with the continuing religious divisions in England, executed both evangelicals and traditionalists. In 1540, he again pressed his more conservative view of the Church and the sacraments on convocation and Parliament. His leadership of the Church created the confusion, as he selected which doctrines, worship, and practice to impose on the people, never satisfying either the Catholics or the Protestants. It was his legacy that the government should decide religious questions and enforce its decisions.

Toward the end of his reign, Henry VIII seemed to govern by contradictory impulses: he argued for religious uniformity in his kingdom and maintained religious diversity at his court. Thomas

Cranmer, the Lutheran Archbishop of Canterbury, and Stephen Gardiner, the Catholic Archbishop of Winchester, engaged in a struggled to influence the king, who seemed to favor first one, then the other. Both had served him well in the past in the matter of the divorce from Catherine of Aragon and the break from Rome.

Henry also continued to pursue diplomatic efforts that tilted him now to Cranmer and now to Gardiner—war with France and Scotland and alliances with Spain or Germany could require adjustments in his religious policy at home. In 1544, Henry went to war again in France, and again put great stress on the English economy. Therefore, in 1546, the Chantries Act seized the wealth of these chapels established to offer Mass for the dead. As the dissolution of monasteries in the late 1530's had done, so now this move put some money in the royal coffers without having to go into debt to Belgian bankers or continue exorbitant taxation and the debasement of coin, which caused inflation and other economic woes.

On Christmas Eve, 1545 Henry gave his last speech to Parliament. He begged the members again to be more united, more centered on his religious settlement. Gardiner's more conservative faction took this as a signal to have Queen Catherine Parr arrested on charges of heresy. She had adopted more evangelical views, and had even argued theology with Henry. He seemed to go along with the plans to arrest her, but she was able to mollify him with the excuse that she discussed religion to provide distraction for him and education for herself. Abruptly changing his mind about her heretical views, Henry nevertheless did not stop the process, but was there with the Queen to shame Thomas Wriothesley, his Chancellor, when he attempted to arrest her. He had also permitted plans to arrest Cranmer to go forward and acted similarly in that case, too, forgiving Cranmer and disconcerting those he had ordered to arrest him.

Playing the two sides against each other was hardly the way to the unity and uniformity he wanted. Henry was adamant that both those who denied the Real Presence in the Eucharist and those who denied his supremacy in the Church were to be executed for heresy. Robert Hutchinson suggests that Henry was responsible for "the judicial murder of up to 150,000 of his hapless subjects."[15] The number is "extrapolated from reports on executions from available monthly county assizes throughout the reign and those who were killed for treason or heresy, or who died during insurrection and other civil disturbances" which, like the Pilgrimage of Grace, were often sparked by Henry's religious policies.

As Henry became less and less able to manage the business of ruling, he transferred the power of his signature to others. The conservative Catholic wing found themselves out of favor and unable to contact or influence the king. Edward Seymour and John Dudley moved against their rival, Thomas Howard, Duke of Norfolk (uncle of both Anne Boleyn and Catherine Howard) and his son, Henry Howard, Earl of Surrey, accusing them of treason. With Henry's approval, Surrey was executed; Norfolk was still in the Tower when Henry died.

At his death in 1547 Henry left provisions in his will to have Masses said for the repose of his soul and for alms to poor people on condition that they pray for him. Although Henry had forbidden the teaching of the doctrine of purgatory, he was unwilling to die without assurance of the prayers of the saints in heaven and the Church on earth, "that he might 'sooner gain everlasting life.'"[16] It was one more sign of the confusing legacy of Henry VIII. These bequests remained unfulfilled, as the evangelical party was ready to seize power. Led by the new king's uncles, the Seymours, this group launched a more radical reformation that Henry VIII would not have permitted.

Winston Churchill sums up Henry's reign as one of great achievement in parliamentary development. He also commends Henry for maintaining order and discipline in England without a standing army. Against these virtues, he deplores as "a hideous blot upon his record" and a "brutal sequel to the bright promise of the Renaissance" the executions of "two queens, two of the King's chief Ministers, a saintly bishop, numerous abbots, monks, and many ordinary folk" and "almost every member of the nobility in whom royal blood ran."[17]

Henry created confusion in the lives of the people of England. Imagine a boy named John and a girl named Mary born in 1509, at the beginning of Henry VIII's reign. They would have lived in a traditional Catholic culture until they were 26. They would have received the sacraments, gone to confession, attended Mass, learned their prayers and the Ten Commandments, celebrated the seasons of the liturgical year, and participated in parish festivities, just as their parents and their grandparents had done. Then came the religious changes of the next 12 years of John's and Mary's lives, from 1535 to 1547. The monasteries were dissolved and the word purgatory was banished, yet a celibate clergy and prayer for the dead remained. Some parish priests introduced Protestant practices and teaching. Others adamantly defended traditional Catholic worship and doctrine.

News from the court of Henry VIII was equally confusing for Mary and John. First Catherine of Aragon was queen, then Anne Boleyn; first Mary was heir, then Elizabeth, then Mary again. When Prince Edward was born and Queen Jane died, these two would have first rejoiced and then mourned. Three more wives would come and go until the death of Henry VIII after 38 years on the throne.

The religious practices of the people of England were now totally bound up in the will of their rulers. Where once there had been two great powers responsible, respectively, for secular and religious matters—the state and the church—now there was only one, the state that controlled the church.

CHAPTER

Edward VI and the Protestant Reformation in England, 1547 to 1553

THE HISTORICAL DEBATE AND THE EDWARDINE PROTESTANT REFORMATION

THERE IS a vigorous historical debate about how the Reformation happened in England and how it was received. Rosemary O'Day, in a 1986 book *The Debate on the English Reformation*, highlights some of the crucial issues. The debate is summed up in two views: the bottom-up theory and the top-down theory. The bottom-up theory, held by historians like G. R. Elton and A. G. Dickens, views the English Reformation as something that needed to occur, an event driven by peoples' dissatisfaction with the Roman Catholic Church, which just happened to be augmented by Henry VIII's argument with the Pope over his marriage to Catherine of Aragon. The top-down theory, put forward by historians like Eamon Duffy, Christopher Haigh, and John Scarisbrick, views the English Reformation as an event that would not have happened except for Henry's argument with the Pope, encouraged and promoted by Protestants like Thomas Cromwell and Thomas Cranmer who helped Henry get his own way. Catholics loyal to the Pope, like Thomas More and John Fisher, did not help Henry do that, so he removed them from the scene.

Neither of these theories can be absolutely true. If the bottom-up theory is completely accurate, Henry VIII would not have blocked Cromwell and Cranmer's more radical reforms. It would have been hard to have a grassroots Reformation movement when England was not a democracy, and, as Clare Asquith notes, "England was not a free society."[18] During the Pilgrimage of Grace especially, Henry was not particularly responsive to the needs and desires of his people. None of the Tudor or Stuart monarchs responded to the minority's needs. Indeed, they often ignored the majority's demands. As for the top-down theory, it must deal with the inconvenient fact that some English men and women were willing, indeed more than willing, to adopt the iconoclasm and more destructive tendencies of Edward's more radical reformation.

The Whig view of English history, summed up by G. M. Trevelyan, for centuries emphasized that what happened in the past marked progress toward the more liberal, reform-minded, enlightened Whig hegemony in British rule. But the winners wrote the history. The only voices opposing this view were those of non-professional historians like Hilaire Belloc and G. K. Chesterton. Particularly since the 1980s, however, revisionist historians like Duffy, Haigh, John Bossy, and others have written well-documented studies questioning the earlier Whig interpretations of Reformation history. Thus, where Elton and Dickens interpreted the Pilgrimage of Grace as a power-driven conspiracy of English nobles, Geoffrey Moorhouse and Robert Hoyle, basing their conclusions upon contemporary documentary evidence, have shown it to be a grass-roots, religion-inspired movement.

The religious changes made by Parliament are not in dispute; more difficult to measure is how people responded to them. Did they accept them wholeheartedly? Did they reluctantly go along? Did they resist? Doreen Rosman notes some of the difficulties in determining how people accepted the Tudor reformations in her 1996 study, *From Catholic to Protestant: Religion and the People in Tudor England.* We do not have diaries or journals from this era documenting interior dispositions. Parish documentation sometimes helps, because of the costs involved in making the changes that were legislated—destroying, building, replacing, purchasing supplies, etc.—and the time factor in those events. So, for instance, when Parliament passed a law stipulating the removal of altars and the construction of communion tables, it gave parish churches and cathedrals a deadline. The speed with which the work was done, as documented in parish account records of payments, can serve as an indicator of how eager or reluctant a particular parish was to make the changes and how much or little its people agreed. If the work was done ahead of schedule, one can assume enthusiasm for the project; if it was merely done on schedule, this could be interpreted as less than enthusiastic obedience; if the work was delayed or the deadline was missed, it could mean the parish did not want to make the changes, though of course other reasons, such as a shortage of labor or money, might be the explanation.

In his study of the village of Morebath, Eamon Duffy has shown that parishes might even outwardly conform while inwardly rebelling against legislated changes. "Writing about Morebath in 1992," he says, "I had fully grasped neither the fact nor the implications of the remarkable promptitude and punctiliousness of Morebath's conformity with successive phases of Henrican and early Edwardine Reformations (Morebath acquired an English Bible, for example, before many of the urban parishes of Exeter), nor the extent of their conservative loathing for reform." But that loathing of reform, together with the bankrupting financial demands of government-enforced Reformation, led Sir Christopher Trychay, the priest, and the parishioners of Morebath in 1549 to arm and finance five unmarried men of the village "to join the traditionalist rebels besieging Exeter in protest against the Reformation and the *Book of Common Prayer*."[19] Their obedience had reached a tipping point, and they could not conform any more. Only two of the men came back when the rebels lost, while Morebath continued to lose aspects of the community life all cherished.

Another indicator of attitudes and beliefs has been the tracking of wills, legal documents spelling out bequests for Masses and prayers for the dead, donations to churches for candles or other supplies: these can also reveal how widespread acceptance or rejection of the Reformed religion was in England. Throughout the Tudor era, some parts of England, particularly London, more eagerly embraced the Protestant Reforms, while others, like Lancashire or the north, resisted and remained committed to the Catholic faith well into Elizabeth's reign.

Reflecting on successful revisionist efforts, Duffy says "almost everyone now agrees" that although some people were enthusiastic about Protestantism during Henry VIII's years on the throne, there was no groundswell of popular support; yet during the span of three generations radical change in English worship and faith unquestionably took place; and the combination of internal resistance and external conformity remain rather mysterious in his view.[20]

We know for certain nevertheless that under the protectorates first of Edward Seymour, the Duke of Somerset, and then of John Dudley, the Duke of Northumberland, the true Protestant Reformation in England began. This Reformation was more aligned to the Calvinist and Zwinglian Reformation on the Continent. Edward, the boy king, regarded himself as the second Josiah, destroying the idols of Baal. He enjoyed hearing sermons and took notes, especially on the duties of kings, although as a minor he could not yet rule on his own. He agreed with the Reformation as it proceeded in England and sternly urged on its pace. Acts of Parliament decreed that altars be destroyed, communion tables set up in their place, statues and paintings be destroyed, chantries or chapels for prayers for the dead be closed, and bibles and books by Erasmus be purchased (November, 1547).

Although Edward VI applauded the religious changes, he was not yet the reigning monarch because of his youth. His uncle, Edward Seymour, Duke of Somerset, took control of the government as Lord Protector in violation of Henry's will. Within Edward's court his uncles became rivals for power. The younger uncle, Thomas Seymour, Lord High Admiral, wanted power and riches like his brother. He married Henry's widow Catherine Parr, and the Princess Elizabeth lived with them in Chelsea on the Thames. Seymour even attempted to kidnap Edward and marry Elizabeth after his wife died in childbirth. He was arrested, thrown in the Tower, and executed in 1548.

His brother, Somerset, fared no better. He offended most of the nobles with his economic policies and the general population with his religious ones. Trying to fill the vacuum left by the death of a king of Henry VIII's stature, he continued Henry's military campaigns against Scotland and France. Meanwhile the kingdom suffered from

Henry's economic legacy. Bad harvests and negative reaction to the *Book of Common Prayer* added to the unrest. Somerset followed his brother to the block and was executed in 1552.

During the first two years of Edward's minority, there was a transition from the Latin Mass to the English communion service. Then in 1548 Thomas Cranmer's Book of Common Prayer became the guide for public worship, again by an act of Parliament, without any indication that the Convocation of Bishops had approved it. It was not well received, and there were uprisings and disturbances throughout the country—even in London, which was usually more willing to go along, and even to anticipate, royal and parliamentary religious decisions. Many people wanted the Mass as they had known it all their lives, and many of the clergy, despite Archbishop Cranmer's efforts or those of their own bishops, continued to celebrate the Mass of the Old Faith.

Susan Brigden calls their rebellion "a direct challenge to the evangelical revolution which was beginning."[21] The Protestants at court were stunned that anyone should challenge their authority on religious matters. From 1547 to 1553, they implemented a series of changes, ranging from imposing communion under both forms, to the destruction of images and altars and allowing priests to marry—all without ever consulting the Convocation of Bishops—and they were surprised that people did not accept their authority.

Cranmer's *Book of Common Prayer* combined prayers from the Catholic missal (for the celebration of Holy Communion), the breviary (for the hours of the Divine Office), and the ritual (for the celebration of the other sacraments and other services). It was meant to bring uniformity, but neither Catholics nor Protestants were completely satisfied. John Knox, for example, protested against the instruction to kneel before receiving Holy Communion, thinking it too papist. That instruction became known as the "Black Rubric" because the theological significance of kneeling was explained away in black type: kneeling for communion was just a means to make everything orderly, not an indication that transubstantiation had occurred and that Jesus Christ was really, sacramentally present, body, blood, soul, and divinity. Under the influence of Knox, Peter Martyr Vermigli (Regius Professor of Theology at Oxford), and John a Lasco from Poland, Cranmer himself had come to a more Zwinglian or Calvinist view of communion as a mere symbol.

Even though it was not well received, Parliament decreed that the *Book of Common Prayer* would replace all other service books, and that all missals, antiphonals, processionals, manuals, and ordinals must be destroyed. This resulted in the loss of many manuscripts and a continuing iconoclasm, destroying any images by law—except those of kings, princes, or other nobles, as long as they had not been considered saints! Again, the bishops, priests, and lay people demonstrated their disapproval of these government actions, and uprisings took place in Leicester, Northampton, Rutland, and Berkshire, with fights occurring even in the churches of London.

Surely Henry VIII would have been disappointed in the chaos and confusion that surrounded the legitimate male heir for whom he had risked so much. His will had been abrogated twice already: once when his bequests for Mass and prayers for his soul were left unfulfilled and again when Somerset took over as Lord Protector. Although he had set the pattern for the state to usurp the authority of the church, he would surely have not agreed with the religious direction of his son's government; and yet another violation of his will was to come under Edward VI.

MARY, THE MASS, AND CHARLES V

The unpopularity of and the uprisings against the *Book of Common Prayer* did not prevent Edward VI and Northumberland from placing pressure on Mary to observe the new order and give up the Mass. As heir to a king yet in his minority, Mary's ardent Catholicism was a threat and an embarrassment to the religious uniformity Edward's government sought. Mary was still ashamed of giving in to the pressure to swear the oath against her parents' marriage, and she was adamant that she would never give up the Mass. For Mary, the Eucharist and the Mass were the center of her Catholic faith. Like her father she attended several Masses a day (receiving Holy Communion only a few times a year, as was common at that time). She was determined that her Catholic household would have Catholic priests to celebrate the Holy Sacrifice. Charles V, the Holy

Roman Emperor and her cousin, demanded her freedom of worship and even threatened to remove his ambassador and declare war in 1551, a threat Edward's council did not take lightly.

Nonetheless, they continued to harass Mary, so much so that she even planned to leave England. She was packed and ready to meet one of Charles V's agents; but leaving was out of the question, since then, when Edward died and she returned to take the throne, she would be an invader. She could not leave England without the hope of Catholic restoration, and she already feared what Elizabeth would do if she came to the throne. Although her priests and members of her household were arrested and harassed, Mary remained faithful to the Mass, and would not attend *Book of Common Prayer* services.

In the meantime, her half-sister Elizabeth showed herself more willing to conform to Edward's religious practice. She was well received at court, even though Northumberland did not find her as tractable as he required. To Edward, however, Elizabeth was an example of obedience he could use to influence Mary, who carefully argued that during his minority she had to obey her conscience. Indeed, faced by Charles V, even the Protestant bishops of England agreed that it was best not to push Mary too far (though it was sinful to allow someone to sin). Once the Holy Roman Emperor was distracted by wars at home in Germany, however, they pressured her again.

NORTHUMBERLAND'S ATTEMPT TO CHANGE THE SUCCESSION

John Dudley, the Duke of Northumberland did not take Somerset's title, but served as head of the government all the same, calling himself the Lord President of the Council. He changed many of the domestic and diplomatic policies of his predecessor, ending the wars with France and Scotland, and dealing with social unrest with relative mercy, in the realization that the country needed the common folk to raise the livestock and tend the fields. Religious reforms continued unabated, but there was less persecution.

In the fall and winter of 1552, as the king and council were still in the midst of trying to force Mary to give up the Mass, Edward's health began to fail. He suffered from a consumption of the lungs, with painful paroxysms of coughing, fever, and loss of appetite. Now Northumberland feared the loss of power and began to strategize, in case Edward died. He paid court to Mary as the heir, yet began to think of ways to change the succession in his favor and in support of the Protestant reforms undertaken in the recent years. As Alison Weir comments, "Edward's death would put an end to all his schemes, for it would bring Catholic Mary to the throne, and Mary would not look kindly upon a heretic who had bullied her mercilessly over religion."[22] Northumberland also knew that her reign would certainly mean the return of Catholicism, at least in the form her father had commanded, and the reversal of all the Protestant changes he and his predecessor had made through Parliament. So he determined that both she and Elizabeth should be passed over and that the descendants of Mary Tudor, Henry VIII's younger sister, should rule instead. Northumberland settled on Lady Jane Grey, "a fanatical Protestant who would promote the reformed religion, but who was also young enough to be in awe of Northumberland and be manipulated by him," as Elizabeth would never be.[23] Northumberland arranged for Lady Jane to marry his son, Guilford. Thus his son would reign as King when she was Queen, and Northumberland would reign over them both.

Northumberland had to convince Edward to change the succession by making a new will. This was illegal, because as a minor Edward had no rights to alter his father's prescriptions for the succession, which had been confirmed by Parliament. After persuading Edward to make the changes, therefore, Northumberland also had to be ready to take over the government, an action for which he gathered support, even through a secret treaty with the French for arms and money.

Before announcing the death of Edward to the court and the country, Northumberland proceeded to arrange for the coronation of Lady Jane Grey and the capture and imprisonment of Mary. She evaded capture, however, and began to gather supporters around her. The people of England and many of the nobles disapproved of Northumberland's efforts to change the will of their "good king Harry." They all knew that Mary was a devout Catholic, and they knew she was the true successor. Nine days after Lady Jane Grey was crowned Queen of England, she was deposed, and Mary was proclaimed Queen, by God's will, as it seemed to her and many in England. Northumberland had lost his desperate bid for power, and the Council delivered the Great Seal of England to Mary, while sending two members to Cambridge to arrest Northumberland. Lady Jane Grey was imprisoned in the Tower. Elizabeth, who had wisely kept out of the way during the crisis, joined Mary on the way to London, and a Catholic would soon be crowned Queen of England, with a Catholic Mass.

Edward's reign was precarious and brief. His minority status did not prevent his Protestant views from having a major impact on his subjects' lives. In our fictional family, John and Mary's surviving children, Anne and James, experienced decisive changes. English replaced Latin as the language of worship, and the *Book of Common Prayer* replaced the Catholic Mass and the sacraments. The saints' feasts and statues, lives and miracles were removed, destroyed, and discredited. The whole order of worship, and many aspects of parish life, had changed. Soon they would change again.

4

Mary I and Reunion with Rome, 1553 to 1558

MARY'S TRIUMPH

MARY I WAS ENGLAND'S FIRST TRUE QUEEN. She accomplished what Matilda had failed to do, and she possessed more power than Isabella of Castile or Eleanor of Aquitaine, two great women of the Middle Ages. Only her half-sister Elizabeth would surpass her in power and success. During her brief five-year reign, she restored the Catholic Mass, the hierarchy, and England's relationship with the Roman Catholic Church.

Mary Tudor, whom H. F. M. Prescott calls "The Spanish Tudor" and popular history calls "Bloody Mary," came to the throne, after years of neglect and fear, when she was 37 years old—well past average middle age in the sixteenth century. Although Mary had begun life as the precious daughter of Henry and Catherine, and had received an excellent Catholic humanist education, her life changed drastically when her father sought to divorce her mother. Mary then endured separation from both parents. Anne Boleyn bullied her mercilessly when Mary was forced to serve Elizabeth, the new heir. Henry also forced Mary to swear an oath that her parents' marriage was not only invalid but also incestuous. She struggled to remain Catholic as her half-brother and his council tried to force her to give up the Mass and convert to Protestantism.

Another traumatic event for Mary during her father's reign was the fall of her godmother and guardian, Margaret Pole. The life of Margaret Pole (1473–1541) and the fortunes and misfortunes of her family illustrate the dangers of a claim to the throne. She was the oldest child of George, the Duke of Clarence, and the niece of both Edward IV and Richard III. Her maternal grandfather was Richard Neville, the Earl of Warwick, called the "kingmaker." Her father was, according to Shakespeare, executed by being drowned in a butt of malmsey wine. Because her brother Edward had such a strong claim to the throne, Henry VII executed him in 1499 after having confined him to the Tower of London for many years. Henry VII arranged for Margaret to marry Sir Richard Pole, with whom she had five children.

When Henry VIII succeeded to the throne, Catherine of Aragon remembered Margaret's friendship with her while she was in the limbo between Arthur's death and betrothal to Henry. Margaret was godmother and then governess to Princess Mary, and Henry named her Countess of Salisbury in her own right. She held a great deal of land, and arranged important marriages for all of her children except Reginald, who was destined for a career in the Church. Henry generously gave him money for travel and education, and it was even suggested that Mary and Reginald should marry, since he had not yet taken Orders.

Once the matter of the divorce came to the fore, however, the Pole family fortunes became uncertain. Eventually, Margaret was sent away from court, her duties as governess being no longer required once Mary too had been sent from court and separated from her mother. Without seeking conflict, Margaret remained courageously loyal to Catherine and Mary and adamantly true to the Roman Catholic Church. Her son, Reginald, did seek conflict, however, writing Henry to express disagreement with and condemnation of his Supremacy. To Henry, this defiance seemed ungrateful and untimely—and treasonous. Margaret by then had returned to court after the fall of Anne, and she and her other sons suffered for Reginald's attacks on Henry, while he was declared a traitor in absentia. Henry Pole, Baron Montagu, who had been one of the peers at the trial and conviction of Anne Boleyn in 1536, was arrested, attainted, and executed. In late 1538, Margaret too was arrested and held in the Tower of London, where her father, brother, and now her eldest son had been executed—as she also was executed on May 27, 1541, in reaction to further insurrections in Yorkshire and in an exceptionally brutal manner, by an inept axe-wielding executioner who butchered her on the scaffold.

All that she had worked for to create a legacy for her children was lost. Her extensive lands were forfeit to the throne, and only her son Reginald effectively survived Henry's revenge. One of her younger sons, Geoffrey, was also suspected of treason and lived in exile. Reginald, on his part, was proud to claim his mother as a martyr. Pope Leo XIII beatified her; her memorial is observed on May 28.[24]

Knowing what had happened to her godmother and governess, and also to her mother, and how she herself had been treated, how could Mary in confidence work with the nobility and leadership of England?

Her victory over Northumberland and his attempt to change the succession must have been a great personal triumph for her. But it may have come too late. As biographers like H. F. M. Prescott and Alison Weir have noted, the after-effects of 20 years of such horrible treatment did not well prepare Mary to rule. She did not trust her own people; she had to make do with a council including some of those who had harassed her over the Mass and had at first supported Northumberland and the change in succession.

As much as Mary relied on Stephen Gardiner, the Bishop of Winchester, for instance, she could not help but recall his support of her parent's divorce. Gardiner had worked for Cardinal Wolsey during her father's reign to justify Henry's unease about marrying his brother's widow. He was author of a treatise, the "Bishop's Speech on True Obedience," attacking the papacy and supporting the King's Supremacy over the Church in England. Thus Mary regarded Gardiner with some suspicion, even though he had also been leader of the conservative faction at the end of her father's reign and was now her ally in reestablishing Catholicism in England.

Unfortunately—for her and for the prospects of Catholicism in England—the only person she really trusted was her cousin, the Holy Roman Emperor Charles V, who was to influence her rule and her selection of a husband. Charles V was the one person who had stood by her those 20 hard years, and so she still relied upon him.

Nevertheless, Mary began her reign in August of 1553, with a remarkable act of mercy and an irenic spirit. She refused from the start to have the Nine Days Queen, Lady Jane Grey, executed, knowing that she had been a tool of Northumberland. Rare indeed for a king or queen—and unheard of for a king or queen of England—to allow someone who usurped, or attempted to usurp, the throne to live. (Nevertheless, Jane did remain in the Tower under arrest.) Mary was also determined not to compel or constrain others' consciences or force people to go to Mass. But she did want to make sure that those who wished to attend Mass were able to do that; and she scheduled a funeral Mass for her Protestant brother, whose remains had been neglected during the chaos of the attempted coup d'état.

She intended to rule with the advice and consent of Parliament, not as an absolute monarch. Although at first she accepted the title of Supreme Head and Governor of the Church of England, she intended to return that authority to the Pope. One of her first acts as queen was to write to Pope Julius III to ask that the interdict placed on England since her father's reign be lifted and that England be restored to his spiritual guidance.

Mary had many good qualities: she loved children, and was always a kind and devoted godmother; like her mother, she was generous and charitable and liked to visit her people without any pomp or majesty. She was devoted to the truth and wanted to do the right thing. She could also be stubborn—a common Tudor trait—and harsh in her desire for what was right. She had not been trained to rule. The shifting fortunes of her childhood, adolescence, and adulthood had interrupted her education. In addition, she suffered from many ailments, including terrible headaches.

Mary tried to begin her reign justly. She had two goals: first, to reestablish the hierarchy and the worship of the Roman Catholic Church, then, to marry and produce a Catholic heir. She intended to accomplish these goals by following the guidance of Charles V and the husband he would help her select.

MARY'S STRUGGLES

And indeed it may have been Charles's guidance that eventually prevented Mary from reaching her goals. Having delayed the arrival of the papal legate in England, he directed her to a marriage that was unpopular with her xenophobic subjects.

Her English councilors encouraged her to marry an Englishman of royal blood and the Catholic faith. Edward Courtenay, the Earl of Devon, had Plantagenet royal ancestry and had been imprisoned in the Tower by Edward VI because of his Catholicism, and so seemed a likely candidate. His character gave Mary pause, however, as he was immature, impulsive, and proud.

Simon Renard, Charles V's ambassador to England, suggested that his master's son and heir, Philip of Spain, would be a better candidate. Like Elizabeth after her, Mary faced a great dilemma. If she married within her realm, it could provoke jealousy and faction. If she made a diplomatic marriage, it could draw England into wars and alliances that the people would not support.

Even the mere rumor of a Spanish marriage was not popular with either the Council or the people. They feared that England's needs would be supplanted by Spanish desires, and that England's resources would be used for Spanish and Hapsburg wars.

Marriage plainly was essential to the achievement of the goal of a Catholic heir who would displace the Protestant Elizabeth in the line of succession. As Mary continued to weigh her decision on whom to marry, she also worked for the return of Catholicism. Pope Julius III appointed Cardinal Reginald Pole, her cousin, as papal legate to England. Under Pope Paul III, he had been one of three papal legates overseeing the Council of Trent, and later Pole had come within one vote of being elected pope in 1550. He was known as a reformer in the Church, a humanist and thoughtful man, the successor to Thomas More and John Fisher.

Again, the influence of Charles V intervened, as he encouraged Mary to delay the return of the papal legate. Thus efforts to reestablish the hierarchy and Catholic teaching and worship were also delayed. It has been suggested that Charles V wanted credit for the Counter-Reformation in England to be shared with Philip, his heir.

In August of 1553, Mary issued a proclamation to her subjects on matters of religion. She affirmed her Catholic faith and her hope that her people would embrace that same faith. Until Parliament convened, however, she "mindeth not to compel any of her subjects thereunto,"[25] thus fulfilling her desire to rule through Parliament. She did, however, issue a ban on preaching, effectively silencing Protestant ministers. Several bishops, including Hugh Latimer and Nicholas Ridley, and even the Archbishop of Canterbury, Thomas Cranmer, were imprisoned. Mary did not advocate or practice religious tolerance any more than her father and half-brother had before her and her half-sister did after her.

After Mary's coronation in September, the first Parliament of her reign met in October. Stephen Gardiner, the Bishop of Winchester and Mary's Chancellor, led Parliament in the dismantling of Edward's religious legislation in order to restore the situation as it was at the end of Henry's reign. The Queen was thus still the Supreme Head and Governor of the Church, a title she disliked, but the Mass, auricular confession, reverence for images, and prayers to the saints and for the dead were all restored. Parliament also passed an Act of Restitution proclaiming Mary the legitimate offspring of her parents' valid and legal marriage. Elizabeth was still the next in line for the throne, according to Henry's will, but she was not legitimized by act of Parliament.

Mary, unlike her father and half-brother before her and her half-sister after her, actually consulted with the Convocation of Bishops, asking them to advise her on the matters of the Mass and the Eucharist and proper forms of worship. Thus, for the first time, the bishops of England had a chance to debate the issues of the Reformation. They reaffirmed the ancient teaching of the Catholic Church and approved of parliamentary actions to roll back all of Edward's Protestant legislation.

After much prayer and deliberation, Mary finally decided that she would marry Philip of Spain. Her Council was not overjoyed, and her people were not happy. Alison Weir suggests that this announcement set back Mary's Catholic goals: "Overnight, it became patriotic to be Protestant."[26] Renard, representing Charles V, made it clear that the marriage treaty negotiations would allay English fears of a Spanish takeover. Mary would still rule England as Queen after her marriage to Philip.

Northumberland had already been tried and executed in August, 1553 (having converted to Catholicism, perhaps in hopes of being shown mercy), and in November, Lady Jane Grey, her husband Lord Guilford Dudley, and Archbishop Cranmer were tried and convicted on charges of high treason, to which they pleaded guilty. Mary refused to authorize their executions and had them confined to the Tower, hoping for a time when it would be safe to release them. She held this merciful position against the advice of Charles V and her Council.

Then, late in the year 1553, Thomas Wyatt and a group of conspirators, with the support of the French ambassador, Antoine de Noailles, plotted to prevent the Spanish marriage and place Elizabeth and Courtenay on the throne. They contacted both, but Elizabeth wanted no part in the plot, while Courtenay agreed. Elizabeth did not inform the government about the danger to the throne—or her half-sister's personal danger—but avoided any involvement.

In January of 1554, after the Queen's marriage treaty had been signed, Courtenay betrayed the plot to Gardiner, his mentor and friend from their years of imprisonment in the Tower. The government was able to prevent the French aid and quell the rebellion in the west, but Wyatt was still a threat as he and his followers drew near to London.

Mary's courage was evident in speaking to the people of London, comparing their relationship to that of parent and child, and the people rallied to defend her against Wyatt. The speech can be compared to one that Elizabeth would give many years later when Philip II sent the Armada to invade England. These half-sisters displayed the Tudor charm and rapport their father had once had with the people. The rebellion collapsed in London, and Wyatt gave himself up and was imprisoned in the Tower.

This time the Queen could not afford to show clemency to traitors. Reluctantly, Mary signed the death warrants of Lady Jane Grey and Lord Guilford Dudley, and they were executed in February. Lady Jane, the Nine Days Queen, was buried in St. Peter ad Vincula inside the Tower of London, where two other queens, Anne Boleyn and Catherine Howard, also rested. The leaders of the rebellion were also executed, though Mary pardoned 400 of their followers and returned them to their wives and families.

Having survived this threat, Mary was ready for Philip to come to England for their wedding and for Cardinal Pole to return to his homeland. Still concerned about Elizabeth's possible role in the rebellion, she placed her half-sister under house arrest away from the court. Again, her Council and Charles advised against such merciful treatment and suggested that Elizabeth be executed.

Philip and Mary were married at Winchester Cathedral in July, 1554 and Cardinal Pole returned to England in November, after the treason charge against him pending since Henry's reign was dropped by Parliament. The papal legate spoke to Parliament, stressing the need for healing and reconciliation, and asked for the repeal of "all the Acts that remained as obstacles to reconciliation with Rome," except for those dealing with the return of Church land, which would remain with those who owned former monastery lands and buildings.

On St. Andrew's Day, November 30, 1554, Cardinal Pole led a solemn ritual of forgiveness and reunion with the universal Roman Catholic Church and the Holy See. The Convocation of the Bishops participated, making amends for any inadvertent collusion with Henry VIII in naming him "singular protector, supreme lord and even, so far as the law of Christ allows, supreme head of the English church and clergy." Alison Weir calls this "the supreme moment in Mary's life, the triumph that made all her past sufferings seem worthwhile. Now her conscience was at peace; she had done what she believed God wanted her to do, and fulfilled her destiny."[27] The Christmas of 1554 must have been the happiest for Mary since her childhood. She was queen, married, pregnant (like her father, she hoped for a son), and her country was reunited with Rome.

MARY'S SORROWS

Although Eamon Duffy holds that "a convincing history of Mary's reign has yet to be written,"[28] he himself provides some helpful details about the efforts to restore Catholic doctrine and worship during her brief reign. Previous Protestant historians have emphasized that Mary's "Catholic Reaction" failed; Mary and Cardinal Pole had only a short time to rebuild all that had been torn down. The effort began in 1555, and she and Pole died in 1558. There was no Catholic heir to continue what they had begun. Some historians claim that Cardinal Pole, the Archbishop of Canterbury, and the bishops failed effectively to implement the reforms of the Council of Trent, but Duffy calls this an unfair charge inasmuch as the Council of Trent had hardly begun its reforming work by 1555, and the Church in England actually anticipated some of the reforms.

Pole, Gardiner, Bonner, and other bishops had an organized plan for restoration. It required reconstruction, catechesis, reform, and time. They lacked only the time. Among the many sorrows Mary faced toward the end of her reign was estrangement from Pope Paul IV, who hated Charles V, the Hapsburgs, and anything Spanish. Since Mary was married to a Spanish Hapsburg, relations between the Holy See and the Catholic Church in England, so recently reunited, steadily deteriorated.

Nonetheless, Pole began the process of having churches refurbished with altars, vestments, and images. He sent Catholic priests to parishes throughout England. He also convened a legatine synod of the entire kingdom whose

> enactments anticipated what would later be done throughout the entire Roman Catholic world after the Council of Trent. Marian England became the first country to introduce a new piece of church furniture to reserve consecrated eucharistic bread: a container or tabernacle placed at the center of a church's main altar. . . . The synod ordered bishops to be resident, and it also made provision for clergy training schools, seminaries, which would be based in cathedral closes and which would serve each diocese: the first time that the Catholic Church had seriously addressed the problem of equipping a parish clergy to equal the developing articulacy of Protestant ministers.[29]

Pole planned to publish a new and reliable English translation of the Bible, or at least of the New Testament, and started work on a new catechism to be written by a Spanish Dominican, Bartoleme Carranza (which would become the basis for the Catechism of the

Council of Trent). In the meantime, Bishop Bonner of London produced a catechism and collection of homilies for his priests.

Duffy further notes that "the Marian authorities consistently sought to promote a version of traditional Catholicism which had absorbed whatever they saw as positive in the Edwardine and Henrican reforms, and which was subtly but distinctively different from the Catholicism of the 1520s."[30] Pole, Gardiner, and Bonner, knowing they had years of work ahead of them, sought "to reestablish the order and beauty of Catholic worship and the regular participation of the people in the Sacraments, and to underpin it by a regular and solidly grounded pattern of parochial instruction, which would repair the damage of the schism."[31] Cardinal Pole planned to commemorate the return of Catholicism to England every year on the Feast of St. Andrew, November 30, as a way to celebrate the progress and process of repairing the damage of twenty years separation from unity with the Roman Catholic Church.

Historians like Diarmaid MacCulloch and Alison Weir note that the people of England did not immediately return to the practice of pilgrimage and visiting religious shrines, but Duffy suggests those medieval practices were not priorities for the Church. More important were catechesis and the celebration of the sacraments. The Marian authorities focused not on the restoration of Merry Old England but of Catholic faith and worship. Devotions like pilgrimages were of secondary importance next to bringing back the Mass and the sacraments. Susan Brigden, remarking on Pole's zeal for true reform, summarizes the priorities:

> Pole had been one of the most challenging reformers of the Catholic Church, and his vision of a regenerate Church in England was still that of an evangelical Catholic reformer. . . . Pole and the Marian bishops had deeper designs for Catholic reform than the recovery of what was past. They restored only in order to move forward. Pole's insistence was upon scripture, teaching, and education, and upon improving the moral standards of the clergy. . . . The Marian Church laid far less stress upon priestly power and divinely ordained papal authority, and upon the cult of the Blessed Virgin Mary and the saints, or pilgrimages, which had sustained Catholics in earlier times. Yet upon the seven sacraments

they held firm, and upon the doctrine of transubstantiation, they were adamant.[32]

This accorded well with Mary's practice of her Catholic faith. In her dedication to the Mass and the Eucharistic Presence, she resembles her father, for even as Supreme Head and Governor Henry VIII adamantly upheld the doctrine of Transubstantiation and condemned heretics to be burned at the stake if they denied it. For Mary, prayer was prayer before the Blessed Sacrament. She did not practice Marian devotions or visit Marian shrines—or any other shrines, which she did not restore. In this she differs from her mother, since Catherine of Aragon assiduously went on pilgrimages and supported the shrines generously. Mary's behavior mirrors the priority Pole and his bishops placed on refitting English churches for the Sacrifice of the Mass.[33]

To celebrate the sacraments they also had to refurbish the churches. This took money and time. In some parishes, priests or congregants had purchased or hidden chalices, patens, altar linens, vestments, and even artwork, and now they brought them back; but the costs of locating, purchasing, or creating these articles where that was necessary were often burdensome to parishes. Customs of Merry Old England like church ales and other festivities were revived to help pay for the refurbishing.[34]

The bishops were aware of these burdens, but they also encouraged the people to care for the poor. Pole and Bonner, among others, exhorted their priests to counsel parishioners to help the poor through bequests in their wills. But Mary and Pole did not have time to reestablish monasticism in England and restore the monks, nuns, and friars to their charitable roles. Nevertheless, although the government had not demanded the return of monastic lands and structures, it was able to restore the Benedictine Abbey at Westminster and the Carthusian Charterhouse in London. Yet, three years were not enough to rebuild what originally took 300 years to create.

Second only to the restoration of Catholicism, Mary's great hope was for the birth of a son, a Catholic heir to continue the work begun. Twice she thought she was pregnant, but these hopes were not fulfilled. Fearing for the future of the Catholic Church in England under Elizabeth—even though her half-sister seemed willing

to accept the Catholic faith—she became determined to wipe out
heresy during her reign. The Parliament of 1555 revived the heresy
laws as they stood during the reigns of Richard II, Henry IV, and
Henry V to deal with the Lollard heresy. Nearly 300 Protestants and
others were burned at the stake at Smithfield and Oxford in the
last three years of Mary's reign. Some of those executed denied the
Trinity, the divinity of Jesus, or other common and basic Christian
doctrines, others denied specific Catholic doctrines such as Transubstantiation, and still others were guilty of violent attacks on priests
and parishioners at Mass. Some of the Protestant martyrs faced their
deaths with tremendous bravery. Hugh Latimer and Thomas Ridley
famously "played the man" in Oxford, and Cranmer recanted his
recantation of Protestantism and return to Catholicism, thrusting
his right hand, which had signed the recantation documents, into
the fire.

Our modern understandings of diversity and tolerance did not
exist in the sixteenth century. In her day, Mary did not receive the
sobriquet of "Bloody Mary," which was coined in the seventeenth
century after John Foxe's *Acts and Monuments*, or *Book of Martyrs*,
became popular. Duffy cautions against imposing the modern revul-
sion at so many executions to the people of England at that time.
The burnings, he remarks, may have earned sympathy for the victims
without winning agreement with their religious opinions.

The second time Mary was thought to be pregnant, she was
actually suffering from stomach cancer. Her husband Philip had
returned to Spain and Hapsburg wars on the Continent, and Mary
did not see him again. England lost Calais, its last holding in France,
and Mary mourned its loss. "You will find Calais on my heart when I
am dead," she said. She erred in naming Elizabeth her heir too soon,
with the result that Elizabeth was able to take power before Mary
was dead.

In November of 1558, fading in and out of consciousness, she
woke once to find her ladies-in-waiting weeping. She comforted
them, telling them about the "good dreams she had, seeing many
little children like angels, playing before, singing pleasing notes." As
Prescott notes, there was special poignancy in this dream, as Mary
had loved music and longed for children.[35] On November 17, she

heard Mass early in the morning and then died. Reginald Pole died the same day. Now Elizabeth would succeed, and the work of five years would seem to have failed.

Edward VI's minority reign lasted six years; Mary's reign lasted only five. Their reforming efforts—first Protestant, then Catholic—did not have time to take root and thrive. The people of England had endured economic hardship and religious change and uncertainty. As Henry VIII's final heir came to the throne, people wanted peace and stability.

Recall our fictitious family. We can understand their confusion and concern. After the death of Edward VI and the chaos of Northumberland's attempted coup, James and Anne had experienced decisive change yet again. The religious pendulum swung once more, restoring things familiar to their parents but only dimly remembered by them. Communion tables were removed and altars either restored or reconstructed. Candlesticks, chalices, incense, and the Latin Mass returned. During the five years of Mary's reign, they practiced the Catholic faith much as their parents and grandparents and the people of England had at the beginning of Henry VIII's reign.

When Mary died and Elizabeth succeeded her, this family, like others, must have wondered what the government would decide next about religion. Would things remain as they were? Would they go back to Edward VI's ways? Or would the new Queen and her parliament mandate something new? The question that hit closest to home for James and Anne was whether they would be able to fulfill their late father's bequests for Masses and prayers for his soul in the family's parish.

CHAPTER

Elizabeth I and the Final Tudor Religious Settlement, 1558 to 1603

ACTS OF SUPREMACY AND UNIFORMITY IN A DIVIDED COUNTRY

WITH THE DEATH OF MARY and the proclamation of Elizabeth, the Edwardine reformers rejoiced at the prospect of replacing Marian Catholicism with Elizabethan Puritanism. They did not achieve all they desired, and they found out that Catholicism was more strongly entrenched in England than they thought. Catholics briefly hoped Elizabeth would continue Mary's policies, but at her coronation Mass Elizabeth left the service when Bishop Oglethorp of Carlisle elevated the Host. She had Bishop Christopherson of Chichester arrested after his praise-filled eulogy of Mary. When the Convocation of Bishops met in February of 1559, it issued a document affirming the bishops' belief in the Real Presence, Transubstantiation, the sacrificial and sacramental character of the Mass, and papal supremacy. Mary's efforts to restore the Catholic hierarchy had succeeded. Puritan reforms would have to come from the Parliament as acts of state and government, not from the Church.

When Parliament met that year, it passed the Acts of Uniformity and Supremacy. The Act of Uniformity replaced the Latin Mass with the English *Book of Common Prayer* and the Communion Service. It passed by only three votes. The new Church of England was thus the creation of a slim majority in Parliament, against the will of the bishops. The Act of Supremacy declared that the Queen was once again the supreme governor of the Church of England, displacing the pope. She was not called "the head" of the Church of England, but merely its governor. In his study of the relationship between monarchy and religion, Paul Kleber Monod declares this an important point "because it meant that her dominance over the Church's mystical body was political rather than personal."[36]

A royal commission administered the oath of supremacy and enforced the provisions of uniformity. All the bishops but one refused to take the oath, and were removed from their dioceses and imprisoned or went into exile. While only about 200 of the 9,000 priests in England refused to take the oath, the commissioners encountered problems at both Oxford and Cambridge, where the heads, fellows, and officers who refused the oath had to be replaced.

Thus, the state-controlled Elizabethan settlement of 1559 resulted in the complete elimination of the Catholic hierarchy. The parliamentary Church of England was able to appoint new bishops favorable to its doctrine and worship. Elizabeth chose Matthew Parker, who had been Anne Boleyn's chaplain, as Archbishop of Canterbury, although several bishops refused to participate in his consecration.

The parliamentary acts of 1559 meant that for the third time in 12 years, pastors, parishes, and congregants had to change the forms and order of worship. Duffy remarks that people hedged their bets, wondering if everything would change yet again and hoping the old order would continue: wills written about this time included phrases like "if the laws of the realm will permit and suffer the same" with respect to bequests for Masses or gifts to parishes.[37] Throughout England, the new bishops were met with opposition and delay. Even in London, where Protestantism was stronger, the Latin Mass was still popular. Documents from the nationwide visitation reveal the conflict between the Protestant bishops and the Catholic people, particularly in the north, where once the Pilgrimage of Grace had opposed religious change.

But the Elizabethan bishops found that the more Puritan Protestants also were in dissent. They considered the religious settlement too Catholic (or, as they would say, too papist, imbued with too much popery), and they pressed for additional reforms, which Elizabeth would never allow. They protested the inclusion of saints' feast days in the church calendar, and rejected the liturgical form of worship in the *Book of Common Prayer* and the use of crosses, candles, vestments, holy water, and blessings. They also found offensive the "cult of Elizabeth" that developed at court. Elizabeth was honored either as the Virgin Queen, recalling the Blessed Virgin Mary or a pagan virgin goddess like Diana or Cynthia. Her birthday celebrations on September 7 replaced the Blessed Virgin's Mary's birthday celebrations on September 8, and this imagery also insulted Catholics.

We do not know what Elizabeth's personal religious convictions were. She had acted like a Protestant under her half-brother Edward, then seemed to accept Catholicism under her half-sister Mary. Like her father, she opposed both Puritan and Catholic dissent; but she rejected Catholic teachings he would have accepted, especially the Real Presence in the Holy Eucharist. Henry VIII never would have walked out of Mass as she did when the Host was elevated at her coronation. In fact, he would have executed anyone who did such a thing. Nevertheless, Elizabeth wanted the pomp and ritual of the Church of England service, and she did exhibit signs of toleration, such as having the Catholic William Byrd as one of her court composers. Yet she also employed the services of her own pursuivant and torturer of Catholic priests, Richard Topcliffe. Religion was part of her public role as Queen of England. Elizabeth was politic in her expression of it.

Like Thomas Tallis before him, William Byrd (1540?–1623) was able to be both court musician and practicing Catholic at the same time. Byrd grew up singing Tallis's music in the Chapel Royal during Mary's reign. When Elizabeth came to the throne, he left the court for a time to be organist and choirmaster at Lincoln Cathedral. In 1572 he returned and Elizabeth granted him the same patent she gave Tallis, to publish his works. Byrd wrote Latin motets, Anglican anthems, and secular songs. His Latin works include sorrowful motets lamenting the plight of English Catholics. Byrd continued to compose for the court during the reign of James I, but he was also serving the Catholic community with Mass settings appropriate for small choirs of men and women in secret and illegal congregations. Apparently tiring of living a compromise at court, he retired to live outside London.

Because of the surprising strength of Catholicism and the continuing protests of the Puritans, both Parliament and Convocation met in 1563 to strengthen and more solidly establish the newly formed Church of England. The oath of supremacy's range was expanded to schoolmasters, tutors, and attorneys. Convocation approved the Thirty-Nine Articles, carving out what would be called the "Via Media" of the Church of England that supposedly situated it somewhere between Rome and Geneva or Wittenberg—that is between Catholicism and either Calvinism or Lutheranism.

In November of 1569, Catholics in the north of England rebelled, hoping to place Mary of Scotland on the throne. The rebellion was led by the Duke of Norfolk and the Earls of Northumberland and Westmoreland. In Durham Cathedral, the rebels tore out the communion table and replaced it with an altar. Mass was publicly celebrated in the great Norman cathedral once again. After this rebellion was put down, Lord Dacre rose in revolt in January, 1570 but was soon defeated.

In February of that same year, Pope St. Pius V issued the Papal Bull *"Regnans in Excelsis,"* excommunicating Elizabeth and urging her deposition—too late for the northern rebellions and perhaps too bold an action. Elizabethan Catholics now had to choose loyalty either to their Queen or to their Pope. When Elizabeth summoned Parliament in 1571, the age of English recusancy began.

RECUSANTS AND JESUITS

The perceived threat of Catholic disloyalty, caused by the papal bull, together with the reality of Catholic revolt in the north confronted the Parliament of 1571. Acts of Parliament made it illegal to possess any papal documents or any religious objects blessed by the pope.

Throughout the 1570s, Duffy contends, government visitation still found it difficult to wipe out the people's attachment to Catholic images, devotions, and worship. It was an uphill task, with parishioners continuing to hide items from their churches. Elizabeth was not married and seemed unlikely to marry any Protestant prince. Although conditioned to obey authority, people took a wait and see position.

But time, which had worked against Mary's efforts, seemed in league with Elizabethan religious policy. Elizabeth's reign lasted 45 years, more than enough time to stabilize the Church of England and eliminate the widespread memory of Catholicism in England.

Catholics faced fines for not attending Church of England services. By imposition of the Oath of Supremacy, they were being driven out of positions of authority, power, and influence. In addition, priests from the Marian era were growing old and dying. When in 1568 Dr. William Allen founded a college at Douai for Catholic exiles preparing for the priesthood, it soon was filled. Of the priests from Douai, 160 became martyrs in England. The college also began to prepare a Catholic edition of the Holy Bible in English; it was eventually published in Rheims, France (the New Testament in 1582, the Old Testament in 1609).

Dr. Allen then persuaded Pope Gregory XIII to found a college in Rome in 1578. It became a Jesuit seminary where Edmund Campion, Robert Persons, and others were prepared to minister to Catholics in England. In his biography of St. Edmund Campion, Evelyn Waugh stresses the brilliance and difficulty of this undertaking. He also highlights its complete separation from politics: the English priests educated on the Continent never discussed the deposition of Elizabeth. Nor did they have the gaining of converts as a goal. Their purpose was to serve the Catholic population of England.

These young men made tremendous sacrifices. Leaving home and family, they risked arrest and death while hiding and on the run. Writing about a group of martyred priests from Oxford, Ronald Knox described what they gave up.

> When they were up at Oxford the world was all at their feet, and a world which held out greater opportunities, one would say, than our world, for men who wanted to make a name and get the best out of life. They could hope to become paragons of chivalry like Sidney, courtiers like Raleigh, adventurers like Drake, poets like Spenser; or, if they were determined to embrace a clerical career,

there were easy openings for them, and ample emoluments for them, in the Church of England.

But as Knox, a twentieth-century convert to Catholicism, concludes, they instead left home to study for the priesthood and returned home to live "the life of an outlaw" and die in agony in their early thirties.[38]

Pope Gregory XIII, in addition to aiding Dr. Allen and the Jesuits, also mitigated the harshness of his predecessor's document regarding Elizabeth's claim to the throne, advising against any attempt to replace her. Waugh also remarks that Dr. Allen's efforts were particularly important for the future. When finally, in the nineteenth century, Catholics were free to practice their faith, English priests and bishops, not foreign missionaries, were available.[39]

In 1577, the bishops of the Church of England had to admit that there were still more Catholics obstinate in their faith than there ought to have been. In the north, at York, and in the south, at Oxford, the bishops saw what they called popery and superstition flourishing.

In January of 1581, Parliament met and passed a new set of penal laws, making it high treason to be a Catholic priest in England and increasing the fines for not attending Church of England services.

Edmund Campion had returned to England in 1580. Formerly a brilliant Oxford scholar, he had given up everything to become a priest. In his apologetical work "Campion's Brag" he declared his purpose to be serving the Catholic people, not deposing or plotting against the Queen. The Catholic underground had secret printing presses set up to distribute this pamphlet, which then was followed by another, "Ten Reasons" why the English should be Catholic, in which Campion offered to debate Protestant scholars at any time.

Apprehended and arrested, Campion was horribly tortured on the rack, with Topcliffe himself supervising his torture, then offered his life together with ecclesiastical preferment in the Church of England if he would renounce his Catholicism. When he refused he was tried for treason. The man who had been one of the brightest rhetoricians at Oxford and had impressed Queen Elizabeth and her court when she came to visit the university in 1566 now showed his brilliance again. Unable to raise his right hand—

because his fingernails had been torn out—he still ably debated the Protestant divines arrayed against him, and defended himself and the other Jesuits well at trial. But the verdict was a foregone conclusion. Upon hearing the guilty verdict and death sentence, Campion told the court, "In condemning us, you condemn all your ancestors, all the ancient priests, bishops and kings, and all that was once the glory of England." He was hung, drawn, and quartered at Tyburn.

Philip Howard, the Earl of Arundel and Duke of Norfolk (1557–1595), watched the dispute and the trial, and was moved to return to the Catholic Church of his ancestors. This was a very dangerous act, as he had a claim upon the throne. St. Robert Southwell (1562–1595), poet and relative of William Shakespeare, also suffered torture at the hands of Topcliffe and martyrdom for his priesthood. The lives of these two Catholic martyrs, Howard and Southwell, present fascinating connections and parallels.

Both were raised as Church of England Protestants, their fathers having conformed to the state religion, and both died in 1595. In 1584, the same year Howard became a Roman Catholic after witnessing St. Edmund Campion's brave testimony and defense, Robert Southwell was ordained a priest at Douai (where Campion had studied). Howard's conversion had healed his troubled marriage and improved his morals, but placed the Howards in danger at Elizabeth's court. In 1585, he and his pregnant wife Anne attempted to flee England but were arrested. Howard was fined and imprisoned in the Tower of London where he would remain for the rest of his life. In 1588, the year of the Spanish Armada, he was accused of praying for Spanish victory.

Around the time that Howard began his prison term, Southwell began his six years of service to Catholics in England. He was confessor to Anne Howard, who remained staunch in her Catholic faith in spite of the imprisonment of her husband. Betrayed and arrested in 1593, he was held prisoner for three years. Howard in 1595 wanted to see his child, born immediately after he was imprisoned. He was told that he could if he became a Protestant. He refused and died in prison of dysentery.

Both Southwell and Howard wrote poetry, although Southwell was the greater poet. His work was well known and admired by both

Catholics and Protestants. Pope Paul VI canonized Philip Howard and Robert Southwell in 1970 in the group called The Forty Martyrs of England and Wales.

The people of England, sympathetic to the Marian martyrs, were sympathetic also to the Catholic priests and laity so cruelly tortured and executed under Elizabeth. Richard Topcliffe, the Queen's own torturer of Catholics, had mastered his craft, even having a torture chamber in his own home. Imprisonment in a cell called the Little Ease, where a prisoner could neither stand upright nor completely lie down, would begin the torture. Then came stretching on the rack or hanging by the wrists for hours, either of which could nearly kill the prisoner or cause him to lose use of his arms and hands. A priest described his experience of hanging by his wrists:

> Then they led me to a great upright beam, or pillar of wood, which was one of the supports of this vast crypt. At the summit of this column were fixed certain iron staples for supporting weights. Here they placed on my wrists manacles of iron, and ordered me to mount upon two or three wicker steps; then raising my arms, they inserted an iron bar through the rings of the manacles and then through the staples in the pillar, putting a pin through the bar so that it could not slip. My arms being thus fixed above my head, they withdrew those wicker steps I spoke of, one by one, from beneath my feet, so that I hung by my hands and arms. The tips of my toes however still touched the ground; so they dug away the ground beneath, as they could not raise me higher, for they had suspended me from the topmost staples in the pillar.
>
> Thus hanging by my wrists, I began to pray, while those gentlemen standing round asked me again if I was willing to confess. I replied, "I neither can nor will." But so terrible a pain began to oppress me, that I was scarce able to speak the words. The worst pain was in my breast and belly, my arms and hands. It seemed to me that all the blood in my body rushed up my arms into my hands; and I was under the impression at the time that the blood actually burst forth from my fingers and at the back of my hands. This was, however, a mistake; the sensation was caused by the swelling of the flesh over the iron that bound it.[40]

Execution was by drawing, hanging, and quartering. The condemned man was dragged (drawn) through the streets, exposed to the crowd's abuse, and then brought to the scaffold. First he was hung by the neck and cut down while still conscious. Then his genitals were cut off and his body cut open, so that first his intestines and then his heart could be removed. After death, his head was cut off and mounted on a spear, while his body was cut into four parts (quartered) and these parts placed as a reminder of the fate of traitors. The people witnessing these executions would sometimes push aside the guards at Tyburn (near what is now Marble Arch in London) and pull on the priest's legs to assure that he died by hanging and not by torture.

Elizabeth's government depicted the measures against Catholic priests as matters of political security, while the priests argued that they were being tortured and martyred for their faith. The government's position was weakened by the offers of clemency and even rewards if an accused priest would conform and become a priest in the Church of England. Sir Francis Walsingham, Elizabeth's spymaster, disagreed with the torture and execution of the priests, particularly because they died so bravely and gained sympathy for the Catholic cause. He recommended that only a few be executed for the sake of example and that the rest be exiled.[41] Topcliffe's role as Elizabeth's official torturer and pursuivant of Catholic priest was also troublesome for her government, since torture was illegal and Topcliffe became a rather unsavory figure throughout who was accused of rape and other assaults. Various plots and policies of Spain and France complicated the priests' position; even if they were not involved in the plotting, they were spiritual advisers and confessors to plotters, and the government regarded them as guilty by association.

The Catholic laity in England responded to the presence of the seminary priests and the Jesuits by organizing an underground network to guide and hide priests. Catholic estates frequented by Jesuits served as safe houses. A brilliant carpenter from Oxford, Nicholas Owen, constructed ingeniously designed priest holes— hidden passages, panels, floors, walls, and places around fireplaces and large furniture.

Imagine a scene like this. A visiting priest has heard confessions earlier and celebrated Mass; now the household is preparing to break the fast. Suddenly an alarm is raised—government agents, pursuivants hunting for priests, are coming! Amid confusion and fear the priest's vestments and the altar cloths and sacred vessels are put away in a secret compartment and he is led to the priest hole. The home then is searched. Perhaps it is hours before the priest can emerge and make his escape. Some hiding places were almost comfortable, but most often the priest had to stand or stoop silently or even stand in water, nervous and afraid, and increasingly cramped and cold, hungry, thirsty, and needing to relieve himself. The priest hole had to have a good air supply and to be undetectable by measuring or tapping. When Nicholas Owen was captured during James I's reign, he was hideously tortured because the government wanted to know where all those hiding places were.

In *God's Secret Agents: Queen Elizabeth's Forbidden Priests and the Hatching of the Gunpowder Plot*, Alice Hogge records that one of these secret places was forgotten until it was accidentally discovered in the late nineteenth century. In several great Catholic homes, like Harvington Hall or East Riddlesden Hall, which today are open to the public, visitors can see where Catholic priests had to hide in order to be able to celebrate the sacraments with the Catholic faithful.

Catholics who helped hide a Catholic priest in their home were also in danger. Here are three instances.

- St. Margaret Clitherow's husband was a Protestant, but she was a zealous helper of priests, and even kept a Catholic schoolmaster for her children and neighboring children. Arrested and charged with the felony of hiding a priest, she did not plead before the judge in order to spare her children from having to testify for or against her. She was sentenced to death by pressing. She was crushed to death on March 25, 1586. An oak door with more than 800 pounds of weights burst her ribcage and caused death within 15 minutes.
- St. Margaret Ward actually helped a Catholic priest, Fr. William Watson, escape from prison by smuggling in a rope. But he accidentally left the rope behind, and the jailer suspected her. Arrested, she was kept in irons for eight days, hung up by her

hands and scourged. She admitted that she helped the priest escape but refused to reveal his whereabouts. Offered a pardon if she conformed and attended Protestant services, she refused and was hanged at Tyburn on August 30, 1588.

The owner of a home where Mass was celebrated by an illegal priest did not even have to be there at the time to be punished later.

• St. Swithun Wells was away from his home when two priests were discovered there. Upon returning, he was arrested. He told the judge at trial that he wished he could have been present. The judge sentenced him to death by hanging, and he was executed outside his own home on December 10, 1591. Before he died, he told Richard Topcliffe, "I pray God make you of a Saul, a Paul— of a bloody persecutor, one of the Catholic Church's children." But this hope was not fulfilled.

Pope Paul VI canonized these three laypeople in 1970 among the Forty Martyrs of England and Wales.

The laity, however, responded to the penal laws in a variety of ways. Some conformed to the official church and left the practice of the Catholic faith. Some tried to please both the state and the Church. Called Church Papists, they attended the official services while also going to Mass secretly. Some families divided their religious observance, with the head of the household conforming, while his wife remained Catholic and he paid her fines. Fines and restrictions became burdensome, however, and some Catholics found it too hard to be always suspected and subject to search and arrest.

Catholic laymen in England also needed a place to study. The Jesuit Robert Persons, erstwhile companion of Edmund Campion, responded by founding the College of St. Omer, near Calais, in 1594. Until 1762, when the Jesuits were banned from France, they taught the sons of Catholic nobility and upper-class families from England there. Young Catholic men from the American colonies also attended school at St. Omer, since colonial colleges were affiliated with Protestant communities. Charles Carroll of Maryland, the only Catholic to sign the Declaration of Independence, and two of his cousins, John Carroll, first Bishop in the United States, and Daniel Carroll, one of only two Catholics to sign the U.S.

Constitution, all attended St. Omers, even though Catholics in the American colonies faced penal laws just like those imposed by Elizabeth and her successors on those who sent their sons to Catholic schools and seminaries.

As one of Charles Carroll's recent biographers describes the college of St. Omer, it endeavored to "cultivate the whole man in preparation for moral, political, and intellectual leadership," as the Jesuits "sought to train secular leaders" while also working for the conversion of England to Catholicism. The college motto was *"Iesu, Iesu, converte Angliam, fiat, fiat!"* ("Jesus, Jesus, let England be converted, let it be done, let it be done"), and the exiled English Jesuits formed there an "intellectual center of opposition to the Reformation."[42] Even after the suppression of the Jesuits, the Church in France kept the school active until the French Revolution. But the college closed in 1793, and, after imprisonment by the revolutionary government, the students and faculty fled to England in 1795. A new college, Stonyhurst, was established in Lancashire, where the Catholic population was large enough to practice the faith more freely. It is an irony of history that a French establishment for English refugees was thus reborn in England for refugees from France.

The activities and martyrdoms of the seminary priests and Jesuits kept Catholicism alive in England. Unfortunately, schemes to replace Elizabeth with Mary, Queen of Scots, like the Throckmorton plot of 1584, had the effect of linking religious identity as a Catholic with treason. Sometimes, too, conflict between the seminary priests and the Jesuits on means and goals of the mission in England hampered their common efforts. Nevertheless, their mere presence in England was troublesome to Elizabeth's government.

In 1585, Parliament met again to pass additional laws against Catholic priests, singling out Jesuits and English citizens studying for the priesthood on the Continent. Laws also targeted the Catholic laity who sent their children abroad without special permission or who sheltered a priest or knew a priest was in England and did not report it. During Elizabeth's reign, Catholic meant traitor, and international politics impinged on private religious practice while religion affected international policy and war.

WARS AGAINST IRELAND AND SPAIN

The division between Catholic and Protestant determined Elizabeth's foreign policy as it did her domestic policy. She wanted to eradicate Catholicism from Ireland because it was an obstacle to conquest and control, and to support Protestantism in Scotland and on the Continent in order to increase her diplomatic strength against the Catholic powers. Through her reign, Elizabeth was a Protestant queen dealing with Catholic kings in France and Spain.

Whenever the question was raised of her marrying, as her half-sister before her had done, she faced the problem of marrying too far above her, so that her husband would take control, or too far below her, so that the husband would contribute nothing to securing her reign and would even provoke jealousy and division. Elizabeth could look only to Catholic princes as viable possibilities, as there were no Protestant rulers of a rank equal to hers. This explains why she remained the "Virgin Queen"—but that itself also meant the succession was always in doubt. The issue of succession also required that Elizabeth's foreign policy be a difficult balancing of pro-Protestant and anti-Catholic diplomacy and war. If she went too far one way, the Catholic nations were more liable to attack; if too far another way, the Protestants in England would be angry.

In the midst of this diplomatic tangle, England, like other Protestant countries, did not adopt the Vatican's 1582 reform of the Julian calendar, which produced the Gregorian calendar. The Vatican's purpose was to assure that Christians celebrated Easter at the right time (on the first Sunday after the first full moon on or after the spring equinox) in accord with the Council of Nicaea. For 170 years until 1752, during the reign of George II, England had a different calendar from that of France, Italy, Spain, Holland, Poland, and Portugal. The main obstacle to reform was that Pope Gregory XIII had proposed it, issuing a papal bull that under England's recusancy laws it was illegal to possess. Elizabeth herself was open to adopting the Gregorian calendar, but the bishops of the Church of England refused. Protestants and Catholics seemed fated to be divided on everything, including the celebration of the Paschal

Mystery! Even in 1752, when the people of England lost eleven days overnight while finally changing over to the Gregorian calendar, there was some consternation.

Upon Elizabeth's accession, the Parliament of Ireland passed the same Acts of Uniformity and Supremacy. England's hegemony in Ireland was tentative, however. The Irish bishops would not take the oath, and the Irish lords refused and rebelled. Catholicism was the religion of the majority, so that the Elizabethan Parliament and governors were never able to force the Protestant faith on the Catholic Irish. Diarmaid MacCulloch comments: "In no other polity where a major monarch made a long-term commitment to the establishment of Protestantism was there such a failure."[43] In spite of all the government's efforts—martial law, torture, execution, and government visitation—religious zeal in Ireland was Catholic during Elizabeth's reign.

The Munster rebellion of 1579, crushed in 1583, was aided by Spanish and Italian forces. Elizabeth's governor instituted a plantation policy, taking land from the Catholic rebels and giving it to loyal Protestant colonists. In 1595, Hugh "The O'Neill," Earl of Tyrone in Ulster, along with Red Hugh O'Donnell, led a rebellion that occupied English forces until 1603, the year of Elizabeth's death.

Wars and constant unrest in Ireland hampered Elizabeth's efforts to support Protestantism in the Netherlands, then part of the Hapsburg empire. Philip II, Elizabeth's former brother-in-law, was dedicated to bringing Catholicism back to England as in his wife Mary's reign. The war between England and Spain escalated through English privateer attacks on Spanish vessels by Sir Francis Drake and Sir John Hawkins. But England did not have the money or forces to directly engage the Hapsburg empire.

In Scotland, Elizabeth supported those Protestant lords who rebelled against Mary of Guise, regent for her daughter Mary. She promised them aid, but Mary of Guise died before they needed her assistance. Scotland had previously been allied with France, and Elizabeth was eager to see the Scots independent of that Catholic nation.

THE RIVAL QUEEN: MARY OF SCOTLAND

Throughout much of her reign, another Queen, who was her cousin and a Catholic, always posed a threat to Elizabeth. Mary, the Queen of Scotland, was crowned and anointed in 1542 when she was six days old. She was the legitimate heir of James V and daughter of Mary of Guise, from one of the great French royal families. James V was the son of James IV of Scotland and Margaret Tudor, Henry VII's eldest daughter. Henry VIII, however, had placed the heirs of his younger sister, Mary, ahead of Margaret's offspring (thus the claim of Lady Jane Grey in 1553).

Henry had also wanted Mary, Queen of Scots, to marry his heir Edward VI and thus unite the two kingdoms. But James V, maintaining the traditional alliance with France, arranged her marriage with Francois, the dauphin, son of Henri II and Catherine de Medici. Henry VIII's response to this intransigence was called "The Rough Wooing" as his forces pillaged along the Scottish border. When Henri II died in a jousting accident in 1559, Francois became King and Mary Queen Consort of France. Francois died in 1560, and so did Mary of Guise, who had been acting as her daughter's regent in Scotland.

In 1561, at the age of 18, Mary returned to rule in her own right. By now Scotland had become Protestant, with the help of John Knox, who had been unwelcome in England since the appearance in 1558 of his undiplomatically titled *First Blast of the Trumpet Against the Monstrous Regiment of Women*. Although he tried to tell Elizabeth that it was aimed at the regent and the Queen of Scotland, he railed at her own rule as unnatural and found it politic to go to Scotland. There he became leader of the reformers against the regent, arousing crowds to desecrate churches and raze monasteries. In 1560, when Mary of Guise died, the Parliament of Scotland swept away Catholicism and established a Presbyterian form of church as the official religion. Knox formulated the confession of faith and the constitution of the new church—the Kirk—in the *First Book of Discipline*.

Even though Scotland was Protestant and Mary was Catholic, all she required was that she be able to hear Mass. She even tried to discuss religion with John Knox in a few interviews. She maintained, however, that she was not only Queen of Scotland, but also the rightful and legitimately born Queen of England. Her fascinating and charming presence—she was the great beauty of Europe—so near at hand was a great danger to Elizabeth, since proximity made her a likely focus for conspiracy and plotting.

Elizabeth tried to diffuse the danger by arranging a marriage between Mary and Robert Dudley, the Earl of Leicester. Dudley, Elizabeth's favorite courtier, could have been a contact for her in Scotland and an influence on Mary. But Mary eventually married a Catholic Englishman, Henry Stuart, Lord Darnley, and bore a son, who was named James and would rule Scotland—a cradle king—as James VI.

Mary soon embroiled herself in a domestic and moral scandal that led to the loss of her throne and separation from her infant son. She was implicated in the murder of Lord Darnley and then married the Earl of Bothwell, his suspected murderer. She fled Scotland in May of 1568 and sought refuge and aid from Elizabeth.

Elizabeth then held her prisoner for 21 years. Elizabeth appointed the Count and Countess of Salisbury to house Mary securely and in keeping with her status as a queen, which destroyed their marriage and nearly wrecked their fortune. Mary still pressed her rights to the English throne and appealed to the Catholics of Europe to save her. The Throckmorton Plot in 1583 did not implicate her, but she did know about the Babington conspiracy of 1586, which called for invading England, assassinating Elizabeth, and placing Mary on the throne.

Mary was tried at Fotheringay Castle and found guilty, but Elizabeth could not give the order to have a sovereign queen executed, even though Parliament presented a petition from both Houses to have the sentence carried out and the danger removed. On February 8, 1587, Mary was finally beheaded. She portrayed her execution as a martyrdom for the Catholic cause, pointedly refusing the prayers of a Protestant minister and praying for Elizabeth and for her own soul in Latin, a language that, she said, she and God understood. It took three blows of the ax to sever her head. The executioner held it up by the hair, not realizing Mary had worn a wig, and her head fell out onto the scaffold. Her little terrier whimpered and barked amidst the blood until he was carried away.

Elizabeth also understood what Mary's gestures meant—and how damaging these events were in the court of public opinion—and her rage at her council for taking a decision she could not take lasted for months. Susan Brigden writes, "Mary's death removed the menace of a queen-in-waiting within England, but brought new danger. With the succession still unsettled, the old questions of religion and allegiance were laid bare. English Protestants could now support the succession of James VI of Scotland, the Protestant king of a Protestant country, but to English Catholics he was a heretic and intolerable as king. Philip of Spain had been planning an invasion to place Mary [of Scotland] upon the throne: hers was the right and she was a Catholic who would restore England to Rome."[44]

With Mary's death, Philip's dispatching of the Armada by sea to invade England had an air of revenge against Elizabeth. Bad luck and English tactics defeated his great fleet of 130 ships, 18,000 soldiers, and 7,000 sailors. Many of the ships crashed on the coasts of Ireland, where the Spanish found Latin-speaking, Catholic-educated Irish to assist them.

After the Armada, whose defeat brought only a temporary halt in the war between England and Spain, Catholics knew no peace. Once again they were suspected of treason. Within three days of the defeat of the Armada, six priests and eight laymen, already in prison, were executed, and 31 were put to death by the end of 1588.

During Elizabeth's reign, 189 Catholics, 128 of them priests, were martyred for their faith. Nonetheless, 360 priests still served Catholics in England. Catholicism was still strong in Lancashire, Cheshire, and Sussex, and still a danger to the state that continued to be practiced, despite fines, searches, arrests, torture, and death. In 1603, the prisons were full of Catholic priests and laymen. Often, however, being in prison was actually useful for their work. Under the English prison system, a prisoner with money could buy services and privileges and receive visitors. Some priests converted fellow prisoners; they certainly celebrated Mass and the sacrament of confession. Priests were also held in internment camps throughout England.

The last priest to die under Elizabeth was Blessed William Richardson, who had studied in Rheims, France, and in Valladolid and Seville, Spain. Before being tortured and executed at Tyburn on February 17, 1603, he prayed for her. She died on March 23, less than five weeks later.

The wars in Ireland, the chaos there, and the conflict at court with her last favorite, the Earl of Essex, consumed Elizabeth's last years. By the time Hugh O'Neill negotiated peace in 1603, she was dead. Even though the Gaelic lords of Ireland had lost, England had achieved only a political and military victory, as the spirit of Catholic Ireland survived.

Unlike her half-sister Mary, who 45 years before had consoling dreams of angels, children, and music, nightmares made Elizabeth afraid to sleep as she approached death. Near the end she was speechless and could barely signal her agreement that James VI of Scotland succeed her.

When the news of Elizabeth's death reached Ireland, "the towns of Munster expelled the established clergy, tore up the service books, and installed outlawed Catholic priests to provide public celebration of Mass."[45] The last heir of Henry VIII was dead and the dynasty was spent.

Before leaving the reign of Elizabeth I, we should recall the flowering of English literature during her reign. The works of Edmund Spenser, Sir Philip Sidney, Ben Jonson, and many other poets and dramatists bolstered Gloriana's reign and defended the Elizabethan settlement of church and state.

Among the great poets and dramatists of the era is, of course, William Shakespeare, who might have been a Roman Catholic. The debate about the Bard's religion has lately been almost as heated as the debate about whether the author of *The Taming of Shrew*, *Hamlet*, *Henry V*, the Sonnets, and many other works was the William Shakespeare of Stratford-on-Avon or the Earl of Oxford using that alias. That one who seemed to express the glories of Protestant England was in fact an enemy of the state—as a Catholic then would willy-nilly have been considered—seems unacceptable at first. Since England was Protestant, and Shakespeare is England's national poet, Shakespeare must have been Protestant.

Formerly on the fringes of Shakespeare scholarship, the idea that Shakespeare was a Catholic nevertheless has moved to the center.

Shakespeare was certainly born and raised in a Catholic milieu. Members of his family, notably his father and daughter, were recusant Catholics who refused Church of England oaths and sacraments. There were contemporary reports that Shakespeare died a Papist. Authors ranging from Peter S. Milward, S.J. (*Shakespeare the Papist; The Catholicism of Shakespeare's Plays*) and Stephen Greenblatt (*Hamlet in Purgatory*) to Clare Asquith (*Shadowplay: The Hidden Beliefs and Coded Politics of William Shakespeare*) see in his works signs of Catholicism either as art, theme, or secret code.

Biographers have also investigated this question. The series of biographies focused on Shakespeare's Catholic connections began in 1968 with John Henry de Groot's *The Shakespeares and the Old Faith*. In *Shakespeare: The Lost Years*, E. A. J. Honigmann presents the theory that the young Shakespeare lived with a recusant family in Lancashire. Michael Wood, in his popular study *In Search of Shakespeare*, firmly identifies Shakespeare and his family with two Catholics martyrs: Edmund Campion and Robert Southwell. In one of the latest biographies, *Will in the World: How Shakespeare Became Shakespeare*, Stephen Greenblatt concludes that whatever faith William Shakespeare had, he turned to the theatre to fulfill people's needs for ritual and community,[46] which had been taken away by what Eamon Duffy calls the stripping of the altars.

Shakespeare was not a favorite of Elizabeth I, even though she did ask for another appearance of Falstaff after the *Henry IV/Henry V* cycle of plays. The Earl of Essex arranged to have Shakespeare's *Richard II* performed the night before his planned coup. Elizabeth knew the significance of the play, which depicts the forced abdication of Richard in favor of Henry IV. "Know you not, I am Richard II?" she told one of her counselors. Shakespeare would have better luck under James I, writing *Macbeth* in honor of the new king.

Throughout Elizabeth's reign, the uncertainty of the succession cast a shadow upon the achievements of the Elizabethan Settlement. Her long reign helped stabilize the Church of England as a compromise between Puritanism and Catholicism, but she and her government could never dispatch either dissident group. Elizabeth kept Puritans out of influence in the Church of England, but she failed to keep Catholic priests out of England. She failed to convert Ireland or to eradicate Catholicism there. Especially towards the end of her reign, an uncertain succession raised the hopes and concerns of both the Puritans and the Catholics.

Catholics had also struggled with many choices during the reign of Elizabeth. As English, they were loyal to their sovereign. In spite of the papal bull, they still believed she had rightful authority. Yet the Queen they wanted to support would not let them practice their religion; and for them to do so meant disobeying her will. Catholics in England might indeed have benefited by Mary, Queen of Scots' coup d'état or the success of the Spanish Armada. Most, however, wished to be able to practice their faith without political revolution. Suffering mistrust, persecution, and prosecution as one regime drew to an end, they hoped for an improvement in their situation under a new one.

Elizabeth's 45-year reign brought stability but not always unity. The children of our fictional family, James and Anne, had married and raised their own children. James married a woman named Catherine, Anne a man named Henry. Their children grew up in the Anglican Church of England, familiar with the *Book of Common Prayer*, bishops, and decorous worship, as Elizabeth required.

James and Anne could not fulfill their father's bequests for Masses and prayers for his soul, since the new religious settlement forbade it. They and their spouses faced momentous decisions as parliament passed round after round of recusancy laws. Supposing Anne's husband Henry to have been a schoolmaster or tutor, he would have to take the Oath of Supremacy. Hearing about the rebellions in the North of England in 1569 and 1570, all were shocked to learn of Pope Pius V's bull excommunicating Elizabeth and dividing Catholic loyalty between sovereign and Church. Henry had to conform to keep his job. Anne might have remained upset over her inability to carry out her father's last will and testament, and might have refused to attend the Church of England, instead taking advantage when possible of secret visits of a Jesuit or other priest to their town. She would have agreed with Cecily Stonor, who testified at her recusancy trial at Oxford in 1581:

> I was born in such a time when holy mass was in great reverence, and brought up in the same faith. In King Edward's time this reverence was neglected and reproved by such as governed. In Queen

Mary's time, it was restored with much applause; and now in this time it pleaseth the state to question them, as now they do me, who continue in this Catholic profession. The state would have these several changes, which I have seen with mine eyes, good and laudable. Whether it can be so, I refer it to your Lordships' consideration. I hold me still to that wherein I was born and bred; and so by the grace of God I will live and die in it.[47]

James and Catherine went along with the changes, attended Anglican services, although James retained an undemonstrative loyalty to the faith of his father and mother. As time passed, recusancy laws strengthened, fines increased, and Jesuits and the laity who helped them were arrested and executed, pressure grew on Anne to conform. Her adamant loyalty placed the family under suspicion and even put it in danger. When Anne died, by the grace of God in the faith wherein she was born and bred, the last link to the faith their ancestors had known was gone.

For the children, the only Church was the Church of England. Anne's clinging to the Roman Catholic Church was an embarrassment. To her grandchildren, Catholicism was something foreign, dangerous and strange, associated in their minds with Bloody Mary, the Spanish Armada, and plots to put Mary, Queen of Scots on the throne.

As the great-grandchildren of John and Mary heard of the death of Elizabeth and the succession of James Stuart of Scotland, they hoped for a smooth transition from one dynasty to another, with no revolution in either church or state. Their grandparents and parents had surely seen enough change.

2
PART

Stuart Revolutions and Religious
Settlements from the Seventeenth
Century to the Twentieth

CHAPTER

James VI and I:
No Bishop, No King, 1603 to 1625

INTRODUCTION TO THE STUART DYNASTY

THE TRANSITION FROM TUDORS TO STUARTS brought many changes for England. For the first time in hundreds of years, a foreigner—a Scot—was coming to take the throne, and he came to rule without conquest. In fact, he was welcome. The English nobility and those at court were tired of Elizabeth's rule. Her last years had been particularly difficult as she aged and diminished. Her image as Gloriana faded, and the ruling classes saw only an old and indecisive woman. (Later generations would value her reign far more highly, and the image of the golden Elizabethan era is secure.)

James brought a family—a Queen to reign, an heir (Henry), and a spare (Charles). The succession was assured, as never through the 45 years of Elizabeth's reign. More than that, a *Protestant* succession was assured. Mary, Queen of Scots, James's mother and Elizabeth's most likely heir for years, was assuredly Roman Catholic; the ruling classes of England had long had the nagging fear that a Catholic would come to the throne and everything would change again. The accession of James I removed that uncertainty. His wife's conversion to Catholicism no doubt was a cause for concern—after all, priests would be at court in her service—but the Stuart children had received a thoroughly Protestant upbringing.

Still undecided, however, was what kind of Protestant succession there would be. James was coming from Presbyterian, Calvinist Scotland to Episcopalian, Arminian England. The Puritans in England had never been happy with the Elizabethan settlement. They had always wanted the vestiges of Catholicism eliminated from the Church of England, including the bishops (Episcopalianism) and the doctrine of free will (Arminianism). As James traveled from Scotland to London for the coronation, meeting with nobles along the way, hunting for hours on end, freeing and pardoning prisoners (except Catholics), England entered a new era. Yet it faced the same religious dilemma, to be resolved the same way. The dilemma was what direction the Church of England under James would take— toward Puritanism or Anglicanism? Its resolution: the majestic will of the king would decide.

Even though Elizabeth's long reign seemed to establish the Church of England as part of the tradition and structure of the land, the compromise of the Elizabethan settlement was still a compromise. The course of the Stuart Dynasty, from the reigns of James I and Charles I through the Civil War and the Interregnum, would demonstrate how weak that compromise was.

James I maintained the compromise by upholding the episcopacy and the persecution of Catholics, while allowing the Presbyterians in Scotland to maintain the discipline and worship of the Kirk. Under Charles I, the compromise would fall apart, for while continuing the official persecution of Catholics in the countryside, he allowed Catholic numbers and influence to grow at court. The Puritans in England mistrusted him. Indeed, he upheld the episcopacy as securely as his father, but he also intruded into the discipline and worship of the Kirk in Scotland. Certainly, these actions led to the Civil War and the Interregnum; but Elizabeth's formation of the Anglican Via Media contributed to the crisis, since it had left unresolved the mixture of Catholic and Protestant influences in the Church of England.

The Stuart era in England can be divided into four stages.

1. The accession of James I and the succession of Charles I.
2. The English Civil War, fall of the monarchy, rise of Parliament and the Puritans; the Commonwealth and Protectorate (the Interregnum, "between reigns"): Oliver Cromwell, Lord Protector.

3. The restoration of the monarchy and the Church of England: Charles II and James II.

4. The Glorious Revolution in 1688 and the Act of Succession in 1701: William and Mary; Anne.

As under the Tudors, so also in the Stuart era the fortunes of the Church of England, of Catholics, and of Puritans or other Protestant dissenters changed as one period gave way to another. At every juncture, the power and authority of the sovereign government determined the religious belief, worship, and discipline of England, Scotland, and Ireland.

The end of the Stuart Dynasty and the Act of Succession of 1701 heralded the coming of the Hanoverians, another line of foreign rulers of England. As we shall see, that transition, combined with Enlightenment rationalism and religious lukewarmness, was to effect some very modern changes, foreshadowing today's secularism in the role of religion in British society. The lesson, to anticipate, that state control—in this case, of the established Church of England—has tremendous consequences for religion, even when the state becomes indifferent to doctrine and worship.

PURITAN DISAPPOINTMENT: THE ANGLICAN CHURCH AND THE KING OF ENGLAND

As James came south from Scotland to reign in England, both Puritans and Catholics hoped for a new ally.

The Puritans held a Calvinist theology of redemption, wanted a Presbyterian structure without an episcopal hierarchy, and rejected state control of the Church. They did not realize that James hated living under the Kirk, the Presbyterian Church, in Scotland. He had studied Reformation and Counter-Reformation theology, and was convinced that the authority of the Apostles had been passed on to the successor bishops. James also saw a connection between the authority of the King and the bishop. Aidan Nichols writes: "As [James] himself said, 'no bishop, no king.' People need fathers and they find them for the nation in the king, and for their souls in the bishop."[48] James exercised his role in the Church through the bishops, approving their episcopal actions and decisions. The

Puritans had been disappointed in Elizabeth's reign because she refused their reforms of the Church of England; now they were disappointed with James's religious policies.

James' Puritan subjects were also disappointed in other aspects of his behavior: his court and his desire for peace, even peace with Catholics. Although they hoped he would reform the royal court, ridding it of pagan masques and celebrations, James' court was soon known for political corruption and luxury. They had also hoped he would not be as parsimonious as Elizabeth with funds for wars against Catholic powers like France and Spain, but James was too peace-loving and tolerant. Like Elizabeth, he was no reformer.[49]

As the seventeenth century progressed, William Laud, Launcelot Andrewes, and others developed a stronger vision of the ecclesiology of the Anglican Church under the influence of Richard Hooker's *On the Laws of Ecclesiastical Polity*. The Via Media outlined in Hooker's seven-volume work gained influence through the reigns of the first Stuarts.

Aidan Nichols notes that Hooker knew no other church than Elizabeth's: "He was not old enough to remember the pre-Reformation church, nor the split from Rome, nor Henry's Catholicism-without-the-Pope, nor Edward VI's Calvinist religious program, not (*sic*) Mary's short-lived Catholic reaction."[50] He set out to defend the Church of England, legally as established under Elizabeth, against the Puritans. Nichols says Hooker's work "presents the Church of England as reformed, yet also the heir to the Catholic centuries" and set "forth an intellectually satisfying presentation of the Christian faith in its Anglican form," while presenting a rationale for a national church.[51]

In James' reign, William Laud and Launcelot Andrewes continued the development of the Via Media conception of the Church of England as a body lying between the extremes of Roman Catholicism and Puritanism. Laud wanted to retain as much ritual beauty and order as possible in the services of the Anglican Church. He also stressed the importance of Holy Scripture and the Apostolic Tradition as the primary norms of faith for the Church.

Like Laud, Launcelot Andrewes referred to the ancient Church and the Church Fathers (identified as such by the Roman Catholic

Church), for an understanding of the Eucharist as both a sacrament and a sacrifice. He celebrated the Eucharist with candles, vestments, and incense—though only in his private chapel—and he corresponded with Robert Cardinal Bellarmine, with whom he found much to agree. The difficult questions with which these Anglicans struggled in their thinking about the Via Media arose from the Tudor compromise wrought by Henry and Elizabeth:

- Was the Church of England Catholic?
- Was the Church of England Protestant?
- If it is neither, what links it to the truth of the early Church?
- How does it know that what it teaches is true?

Since, especially under Elizabeth, the Church of England was established not by the authority of the convocation of bishops, but by the political efforts of Parliament, it was difficult for Anglican ecclesiology to reflect on tradition or the episcopacy. Recall that the Convocation of Bishops before Elizabeth's first Parliament had declared their unity with the Pope in Rome, upon which Parliament dissolved that unity and replaced those bishops. This provided a shaky foundation for episcopal authority, since apparently it was a perquisite of political authority to define the doctrine and practices of the Church of England and say who could be a bishop and uphold that state-defined doctrine.

As John Henry Newman was to discover in the nineteenth century, the authority of the Church of England in the Anglican theology of the Via Media looked good on paper and as an idea, but it was difficult for Hooker, Laud, and Andrewes (and, in due course, Newman) when surveying the history of the Elizabethan settlement, to trace the path by which apostolic authority came to bishops in the Church of England. The Thirty-Nine articles even denied the intrinsic authority of the general councils of the Church. But these Anglican divines ignored that aspect of the Articles, since the first seven ancient ecumenical councils defined and defended the Catholic Church's doctrines on Jesus, Mary, the Holy Spirit, and other momentous truths, and the Anglican theologians saw them as inheritances from the Apostles. Indeed, these councils had defined the very creeds, Nicene and Athanasian, that the Thirty-Nine articles assented to. Thus, the Thirty-Nine Articles embody the strange contradiction of denying the authority of the general councils of the Church while accepting as authoritative the doctrinal statements of those same general councils.

After 45 years of living in the Elizabethan settlement, the Anglican divines of the seventeenth century were still wrestling with the predicament Diarmaid MacCulloch calls "the building of a Protestant Church which remained haunted by its Catholic past."[52] Another description of the Church of England is that was an "inconsistent, disunited ecclesiastical institution" representing the "national Protestant church," which was "quasi-Catholic" while "largely unreformed" (as pluralism and absenteeism were still widespread), with one unifying factor: fear and hatred of the pope and the Roman Catholic Church.[53]

James I was an amateur theologian who enjoyed discussing and debating these issues. He also used preferments and other gifts to build up the Anglican community, encouraging John Donne, for instance, to become a minister in the Church of England.

James arranged the marriage of his eldest daughter Elizabeth to Frederick, the Elector of the Palatine, who opposed the Catholic Hapsburgs in Bohemia. Frederick reigned briefly as King of Bohemia, but lost the crown when he was defeated at the Battle of the White Mountain in 1620. Called either the Winter Queen or the Queen of Hearts, Elizabeth was staunchly Protestant. Her Protestant descendants would provide England with an heir when the Stuart dynasty died out in the eighteenth century. During James I's reign, Protestants in England were supportive of the Elector, but James did not intervene on his behalf with money or troops. Parliament was prepared to fund that support, but made it contingent on ending the alliance with Catholic Spain, something James refused to do. This further upset the English Puritans, for it seemed that James followed a policy of appeasement with Catholic countries and was unwilling to support the Protestant cause against Catholic powers.

In one way, however, James I did please the Puritan party in the Church of England. He did so by his support and patronage of the Authorized Version of the Holy Bible. He was involved in the selection of the scholars on the translation committee, including

Launcelot Andrewes, and he provided some church preferments for their efforts. Known as the King James Bible, the translation's prose style exercised enormous influence on English language and literature. James supported this project because he wanted a Bible in English without the Calvinist notes that opposed his free will theology. In consequence, some Puritans did not trust the King James Bible. Another irony is that the translation committees referred to the Catholic version of the Holy Bible in English, published at Douai and Rheims from 1582 through 1610.

James' efforts in Ireland must also have pleased the Puritans, inasmuch as he gave Protestantism, and specifically Presbyterianism, a foothold there, taking advantage of the power vacuum in Ulster by developing a new plantation plan. After their defeat in 1603, the Catholic Lords of Ulster fled to the continent in 1607. Since they had abandoned their lands, James turned over six of the counties of Ulster to English and Scottish "undertakers" who would displace the Irish, build new castles for strategic defense, and populate Northern Ireland with a Protestant majority. James and the undertakers recruited Anglican and Presbyterian clergy and opened Protestant schools as feeders to Dublin's Trinity College, which Elizabeth I had established.

Like so many other English actions in Ireland, these efforts planted seeds of violence that grew and ripened during the reign of Charles I.

CATHOLIC DISAPPOINTMENT: THE GUNPOWDER PLOT

As James traveled south, another group was hopeful he would help them: the Roman Catholics of England. James had come to the throne because he promised a measure of toleration. Catholics expected some leniency from him because their leaders cooperated with the government in exposing a plot to assassinate him at the beginning of his reign. They also thought that as son of the Catholic Mary, Queen of Scots and husband of the convert Anne of Denmark, James would be sympathetic to them. They did not realize that he had hardly known his mother and was estranged from his wife.

As James prepared to take the throne of England, he wanted a council with the Pope and Puritan leaders to discuss Christian unity after the Reformation. Because the Pope refused to hold such a meeting, James convened the Hampton Court Conference in 1604, with no Catholic representatives invited. The Pope could not send representatives to meet with James because, wily historian and theologian that he was, the King aimed to revive the "conciliar" principle in the Church, and was determined that whatever his council decided, the Pope would have to accept as it applied to Catholics in England. The Vatican could not agree to such an open-ended condition.

Having thought that Catholics were a minority in England, James was shocked, as Elizabeth herself would have been, at their numbers and the number of priests still illegally present in England. When Parliament met in March 1604, James expressed his dissatisfaction with this situation, especially the presence of the Jesuit and seminary priests, whom he accused of trying to win converts. He expressed no anger against Catholic Englishmen, but he deplored their foolishness and rather pitied them. He firmly rejected the Roman Catholic doctrine of papal primacy and urged Parliament to uphold the Elizabethan recusancy laws. He also called for all Catholic priests to leave England immediately or face the consequences.

Parliament followed James' instructions, passing measures that reaffirmed and strengthened the penal laws, with those studying abroad and those who tried to teach the Catholic faith in England the special targets. Those who went overseas to study for the priesthood, obviously without government approval or license, were disinherited. Owners of ships that illegally conveyed these students abroad faced having the ships confiscated. If a Catholic family had a tutor without a license from the bishop, both teacher and employer were subject to a daily fine.

Catholics were understandably outraged by James' betrayal. Although the Pope and the priests in England had forbidden any attempt to overthrow the rightful King of England, some laymen developed a ridiculous and desperate plot to kill James, his family, and the members of Parliament, and seize control of government. Robert Catesby, leader of this plot, recruited several other Catholic gentlemen and Guy Fawkes, who had served in the Spanish army. They planned to dig a tunnel to the cellar under the Houses of Parliament, store gunpowder there, and ignite it on November 5, 1605, at the opening of Parliament.

But one of the conspirators warned a relative not to be there that day. The government discovered the plot, and arrested Guy Fawkes in the cellar, checking on the powder. Government agents tortured him to divulge the identities of other conspirators. These for their part hoped to raise an insurrection in the west, but they were surrounded by the Sheriff of Worcester's posse. Those who did not die there in that encounter were arrested and executed by the end of November, 1605. The government blamed the plot on the Jesuits and executed Father Henry Garnet, who had actually forbidden any kind of plot against the government. If any of the conspirators had confessed their involvement in such a murderous plot, he would have counseled against it, but he could not violate the seal of the Sacrament of Confession.

Seeming again to prove that Catholics were disloyal, the Gunpowder Plot made life worse for Catholics and reinforced the growing fear, hatred, and prejudice. Owen Chadwick says of the anti-Catholic mindset that grew up: "Suspicion of Rome became almost a part of the national character, a part of patriotism, a part of the Englishness of a man."[54] Now Parliament passed a new round of penal laws against Catholics that:

- Increased fines for not attending Anglican services
- Required Catholics to marry in the Church of England or be fined
- Required them to baptize their babies in the Church of England or be fined
- Required the heirs of a deceased Catholic to have him or her buried according to the rites of the Church of England or be fined
- Barred Catholics from serving in the Army or the Navy or as lawyers, doctors, or pharmacists
- Restricted or forbade travel by Catholics abroad or to London or five miles from home
- Made Catholics liable to search at any time.

For years after the Gunpowder Plot, English Protestants celebrated the Fifth of November (Remember, Remember, the Fifth of November!) as Guy Fawkes Day, with bonfires and burning effigies of Guy and the Pope. Official sermons reminded people of God's providential care in saving the Protestant King from Catholic plotting. Prayers of thanksgiving for deliverance from the Gunpowder Plot remained in the *Book of Common Prayer* until 1854. The custom of searching the houses of Parliament before the first day of a session remains a ceremony that tourists can witness to this day.

OTHER CATHOLIC RESPONSES—GEORGE CALVERT, FIRST LORD BALTIMORE AND JOHN DONNE, DEAN OF ST. PAUL'S

The Gunpowder Plot should not be our only image of the Catholics response to the English government's continued desire for religious conformity. Protestant Englishmen, the majority, saw the Gunpowder Plot as confirmation that Catholics could not be good Englishmen. Catholics, the minority, were agitated by the same fears. They desired to be true to both their country and their religion, and the government was making that impossible. John D. Krugler writes: "It made religious decisions public; it denied individuals the right to choose how they worshiped; and it allowed civil authorities to dominate the human conscience."[55]

This tendency to equate being Roman Catholic with having divided loyalties has been visible at times even in the United States, under a federal constitution that guarantees freedom of religion and forbids religious tests for public office. But for Catholics in seventeenth-century England, the simultaneous practice of their faith and participation in government were nearly impossible. Under Elizabeth, Catholics found various ways of dealing with this issue; and the challenge persisted under James I. The Lords Baltimore on the one hand and John Donne on the other provide contrasting illustrations of the response.

George Calvert's family was harassed into conformity to the Church of England when he was a child. Although his father attended official services, his mother never did, so the Yorkshire authorities not only meddled with their Sunday worship but determined what books they could own and what servants they could hire. Additionally, their children's Catholic education had to end, so George and his brother came under Protestant tutelage. When he was twelve years old, Calvert conformed to the Church of England.

He was a protégé of Sir Robert Cecil, principal secretary to Elizabeth I and James I. Calvert attended Oxford and earned his B.A. in 1597 and M.A. in 1605. Becoming private secretary to Cecil, he went on to hold several government posts, each more important than the last: Clerk of the Crown, Clerk of the Privy Council, ambassador to the Court of France, and finally Secretary of State for James I.

Even as he climbed the ladder of public office under James I, Calvert might have experienced pangs of loss and tugs of nostalgia for the Catholic faith when he traveled on diplomatic missions on the continent and worked with practicing Catholics. Nevertheless, he was willing on several occasions to take oaths denying any attachment to the Catholic faith.

He supported the Spanish alliance so dear to James and the marriage of Charles, the Prince of Wales, to the Infanta, Maria Anna. But that match was unpopular, as Mary's marriage to Philip of Spain had been, and its unpopularity damaged Calvert's career. James accepted his resignation from the position of Secretary of State and Calvert declared himself to be a Roman Catholic in 1624 or 1625.

We do not have George Calvert's conversion—or, more precisely, *reversion*—story, but it is clear that he faced a crisis in his personal life before he announced his return to the Catholicism of his early boyhood. His first wife, Anne, died unexpectedly after a difficult delivery in 1624, and he missed her deeply. Then his professional life fell apart. It was only after he left office that he made it known publicly that he was a Roman Catholic.

Because of his loyal service to James I, however, his conversion did not necessarily leave him a ruined man. James was grateful to his erstwhile secretary, and made him a peer in Ireland as the First Baron Baltimore of Baltimore Manor in County Longford. Although James died a few weeks after this decision, the new king, Charles I, upheld Calvert's peerage and role on the Privy Council.

As the first Baron Baltimore, Calvert still had influence and access to the court. He also could pursue economic ventures, especially his project to colonize the New World in the name of England and the cause of religious toleration. Although he died before that project could succeed, he left his son, Cecil Calvert, the vision and the means to accomplish it during the reign of Charles I, as we shall see in the next chapter.

The story of Lord Baltimore shows that Catholics could be loyal to faith and their country. But it was a complicated task. Before his conversion, Calvert had conformed to the official church. James I and Charles I both accepted him as a Catholic, honoring him and even exempting him from the harassment of searches and travel restrictions his parents had experienced, but that was because of his avowed and demonstrated willingness to serve them.

Once Baltimore was Catholic, however, he wanted to find a place where people could be both Catholic and English without complications. His goal was Maryland, which he carved out on the border of Virginia. After the failure of Avalon in what is now Newfoundland, he worked in the last years of his life to obtain a charter for the colony, to recruit Jesuit priests to minister to the Catholics there, and to allow all colonists, whether Protestant or Catholic, to practice their faith. Before Roger Williams had a similar vision in Rhode Island, Baltimore introduced a notion foreign to the Europe of his day: freedom of religion and a nonsectarian government. Not even John Locke, sometimes called the philosopher of liberty, could conceive of such a revolutionary idea. In his "Letter Concerning Toleration," published in 1689, Locke allowed everyone but Roman Catholics and atheists to practice their faith freely. Lord Baltimore was ahead of his time.

John Donne, the Metaphysical poet and dean of St. Paul's Cathedral in London, followed a different path. His family was also Roman Catholic and knew the dangers of being Catholic in England at first hand. His mother, Elizabeth Heywood, was a great-niece of St. Thomas More, and arranged for John to receive a Catholic, Jesuit education. Jasper Heywood, his uncle on his mother's side, had been a protégé of Cardinal Reginald Pole and superior of the Jesuit mission to England in the 1580s. Imprisoned, tried, and sentenced to death, he was exiled instead and died in Italy. John's brother died of the plague in Newgate Prison while awaiting trial for hiding a priest, a crime for which he would have been hung, drawn, and quartered if found guilty.

During Elizabeth's reign, John Donne abandoned the Catholic faith when he was in his mid-twenties. But his conformity to the Church of England did not guarantee his success, especially after the debacle of his elopement in 1601 with the niece of his employer, Sir Thomas Egerton, for which he spent time in prison. Donne tried to ingratiate himself with King James, writing anti-Catholic pamphlets like "The Pseudo-Martyr" and "Ignatius His Conclave," but the king would not give him a court position. Only taking orders brought him material security. As dean of St. Paul's in London, he became the most famous preacher in England. Along with William Laud and Lancelot Andrewes, Donne carved out the Via Media between Puritanism and Catholicism. He was absolutely opposed to the Puritans (as anyone who wanted James' patronage was well advised to be), and he knew Catholicism intimately. Donne was a man in the middle, and it is reasonable to ask how much it cost him to maintain his equilibrium.

Still, there is always a Catholic sensibility and background in his poems and sermons. The experiential focus of his meditations on the Incarnation, Passion, and Resurrection of Jesus betray his Jesuit background and the Ignatian method of "composition of place" found in the Spiritual Exercises. Toward the end of his life, he famously preached and prepared for his death, having his portrait painted in a shroud. A statue of Donne thus garbed occupies a niche at St. Paul's today.

Under James I, Roman Catholic priests were arrested, imprisoned, and executed as criminals. Yet Englishmen continued to travel to the continent to study for the priesthood and returned to England to serve the Catholic people. In addition to the seminaries in Douai and Rome, another of the great English and Irish seminaries on the continent was St. Albans in Valladolid, Spain. Martyrs from this college include St. Hugh Walpole, St. John Roberts, and St. Thomas Garnet, nephew of Henry Garnet.

Since English jails allowed prisoners to obtain special services for a priest, a remarkable Spanish woman named Luisa de Carvajal y

Mendoza (1566–1614) was able to minister to the martyrs of St. Albans before their deaths. She arranged for a last meal and reunion of the priests the night before their executions, when they heard each other's confessions and celebrated their final Masses.

As a member of the Catholic underground in England, this intrepid missionary woman attempted to convert Anglicans. Carvajal was a poet, spiritual writer, and founder of a religious society of Catholic women. She was arrested twice, but the Spanish ambassador managed to obtain her release, since James I wished to maintain peace with Spain and negotiate an alliance. As a child, Carvajal had dedicated herself to holiness and had even made a vow of martyrdom. She died on her way back to Spain—but not as a martyr.

Although James gladly approved of laws against Catholics, he found himself in the same diplomatic quandary Elizabeth had faced. James was pursuing a policy of peace with Spain, and it was hard to negotiate with that Catholic nation while persecuting English Catholics, especially when seeking also to negotiate the marriage of the Infanta of Spain and his son and heir Charles. (Henry Frederick, Charles' older brother, died in 1610 when he was 18 years old.) She would have to be able to practice her faith and would require priests at court to celebrate the Mass and the sacraments. Yet it was illegal for priests to be in England or for English Catholics to attend Mass or receive the other sacraments. Charles and the Duke of Buckingham even traveled incognito to Spain to negotiate the marriage. When they returned, the people rejoiced—they thought the Prince and the Duke had been held hostage. They also rejoiced that the marriage negotiations had fallen through. In Mary's day the people had not wanted her to marry a Spanish prince, and now, with the Armada in mind, they did not want Charles to marry a Spanish princess. They fervently believed the Black Legend depicting Catholic Spain as cruel, superstitious, and tyrannical.

Similar negotiations were required when Henrietta Maria of France, the sister of Louis XIII, was the intended bride. James had to promise leniency to his Catholic subjects so that the Pope would allow a Catholic princess to marry a Protestant prince. James died before the arrangement was ratified, but Charles I began his reign with his marriage to Henrietta Maria.

James I had strengthened the Via Media position of the Church of England against both Puritanism and Catholicism. His doctrine of the Divine Right of Kings meant he could tolerate neither Puritan Presbyterianism nor Catholic papal authority. But James had to contend with the opposition of the Puritans in Parliament as well as the diplomatic exigencies of pursuing an irenic policy in dealing with Catholic nations and rulers. He left to his son the difficult balancing act of maintaining the uniformity and authority of the Church of England in an obviously pluralistic domestic and international environment, guided only by the principle that the King's will, supreme and unopposed, could, should, and would decide what was best for the nation.

7

Charles I, the English Civil War, and the Interregnum, 1625 to 1660

CATHOLIC INFLUENCES AND LAUD'S
HIGH CHURCH POLICIES

CHARLES I FOLLOWED HIS FATHER'S DOCTRINE of the Divine Right of Kings and acted consistently upon it, often in conflict with Parliament. He also continued to support the Arminian (freewill) Anglican party in the Church, where he was even less tolerant of opposing views. Like his father, Charles was married to a Catholic princess, but he allowed even more Catholic influence around his court, and placed Catholics in important positions. There were conversions to Catholicism at court, and generally a more Continental and refined atmosphere.

Charles' tastes in art and music tended toward the French and Continental, and this made him seem almost foreign to his people, whether in England or Scotland. The greatest art collector of his day, he particularly favored two Catholic artists, Peter Paul Rubens and Anthony van Dyck. Catholics were still fined and arrested for practicing their faith, and Charles did not continue the leniency promised as part of the arrangement of his marriage to Henrietta Maria of France. Nonetheless, the Catholic Mass was celebrated in the chapel at St. James's Palace, and his queen, whom he dearly loved, had her chaplains and Catholic household.

Henrietta Maria was an openly devout Roman Catholic, as befitted the sister of the Most Catholic King of France, Louis XIII. She even went on pilgrimage to Tyburn's Triple Tree to mourn the Catholic priests martyred there during her father-in-law's reign. She decorated her chapel in the current Baroque Counter-Reformation style. Her marriage contract guaranteed her freedom to practice her Catholic faith, and she took advantage of that freedom almost brazenly. As Edward VI had thought of himself as another Josiah, smashing heathen idols, Henrietta Maria thought of herself as another Esther, restoring her people's religious practice.

Indeed, she wanted to attract converts among the English peerage, evangelizing through beauty, ceremony, and her position as Charles' well-loved queen. Because Charles loved her so much, many Protestants feared that she might convert even him. He was loyally Protestant, however, and upheld the same beliefs as his father. Growing concerned with the rate of conversions at court and the almost defiant public celebration of Mass in the Queen's chapel, he ordered his subjects not to attend Mass there.[56]

To the Puritans, Charles looked lukewarm in his defense of true, godly religion. His support of Archbishop Laud furthered their doubt and concern. He allied himself with William Laud and the High Church party to eradicate religious dissent and impose absolute uniformity throughout the realm, even in Presbyterian Scotland. Both Elizabeth and James had disappointed the Puritans dissenters, and the Puritans continued their opposition to the Church of England, which they regarded as impure and corrupted by Catholic influences. Charles I's support of Laud and Arminianism reinforced their view, and the Puritans in Parliament dedicated themselves to eradicate the Arminian and papist errors in the Church.

For them, Arminianism was tantamount to Catholicism. Named for the Dutch theologian Jacobus Arminius, Arminianism rejected Calvinist doctrine that salvation was through grace alone and upheld the efficacy of human free will and cooperation with God's grace, including good works. As a member of the High Church party and a believer in the Via Media theology of the Church of England, Archbishop Laud enforced his beliefs on the Church throughout England, emphasizing liturgical beauty and order in the *Book of*

Common Prayer, upholding free will and the community of believers in the Church, and promoting primarily Arminian bishops for the sake of uniformity.

As Archbishop of Canterbury, Laud used the Star Chamber and the Court of High Commission to accuse Puritans of heresy and have them removed from the Church. His policies led to the emigration of 20,000 Puritans from England to the colonies in the New World—until he and Charles realized that the royal colonies were filling up with dissenters and anti-royalists and that property values were being hurt in England. Starting in 1637, only those conforming to the Church of England were allowed to leave.

As the Puritans went to the Massachusetts colonies, they brought their anti-Catholicism with them. Other royal colonies like Jamestown, Virginia, established the Church of England in the Americas and enforced anti-Catholic penal laws. At the same time, Charles had given approval to the Catholic George Calvert, First Lord Baltimore, for the establishment of a colony named Maryland, after Queen Henrietta Maria. This was Calvert's second attempt to provide Catholics a haven in the New World. Unfortunately, he did not live to see its success. Before his death in 1632, nevertheless, Calvert had passed two major milestones toward making his second colony possible: he received a charter for it and he arranged for Jesuits to travel to Chesapeake Bay. Upon his death, his son Cecil became the second Baron of Baltimore and continued to pursue his father's vision. A Catholic convert like his father, he too wanted to prove that he could be both Catholic and loyal to England and the King. In consequence, Cecil had to walk the same tightrope his father had walked.

Founding and funding the colony, recruiting emigrants, and fighting off the objections of the neighboring Virginia colonists were difficult tasks. Maintaining the equilibrium of Catholicism and loyalty to the Crown was delicate as well as difficult. Baltimore wanted Catholics to be able to practice their religion freely, but he did not want them to be so brazen about it that Protestants would complain. Calvert directed that there be no religious tests for public office, and that Catholics, who were the minority in Maryland, not receive preferential treatment. He wanted the Jesuits to help build up the colony and

Above– **St. Thomas More:** "A Man for All Seasons," Thomas More was a humanist, author, lawyer, statesman, and reformer. When he was beheaded on July 6, 1535, he declared he died "the king's good servant, but God's first." His execution shocked the humanist community as Erasmus lamented his loss.

Left– **Blessed Margaret Pole:** Loyal friend of Catherine of Aragon, governess to Princess Mary, and link to the Plantagenet past, Margaret Pole (1478–1541) endured a brutal slaughter by an inept headsman after being told of her execution an hour before. Her son Reginald Pole rejoiced in exile that his mother was a martyr for the faith.

Above– **Campion and companions:** This 17th-century engraving depicts the execution of priests Alexander Briant, Edmund Campion, and Ralph Sherwin on December 1, 1581. Father Briant is speaking to the crowds at Tyburn; Campion is being hung, and Sherwin is about to be decapitated.

Right– **Robert Southwell:** The Jesuit poet received the palm and crown of martyrdom on February 20, 1595. The crowds at Tyburn pressed forward to pull on his legs as he hung to spare him the torturous death of traitors—being hung, drawn, and quartered.

Above– **St. Oliver Plunkett:**
After 25 years in exile in
Rome, St. Oliver Plunkett
returned to Ireland as
Archbishop of Armagh in
1670; nine years later he
was arrested in the frenzy
of the Popish Plot and was
the last priest martyred at
Tyburn on July 11, 1681.

Left– **Mary of Modena:**
The last Catholic Queen of
England, Mary of Modena
gave birth to James Francis
Edward on June 10, 1688
and fled with her infant son
for exile in France five
months later as William and
Mary of Orange invaded to
lead the Glorious Revolution.

Baring/Chesterton/Belloc: Three great figures of the Catholic literary revival in 20th century England. In G. K. Chesterton's words, "Conversation Piece" by Sir James Gunn (1932) depicts "Baring [Maurice Baring, standing], over-bearing [Hilaire Belloc, seated on the right], and past-bearing [Chesterton himself, seated on the left]."

Left– **Richard Challoner:** Richard Challoner served as Archbishop and Vicar Apostolic in England from 1741 to 1781 during the reigns of George II and George III. He wrote many devotional works and revised the Douai Rheims translation of the Holy Bible. He died soon after the Gordon Riots of 1780 when he was nearly 90 years old.

convert the native Indian tribes, but he did not want them to proselytize Protestants too aggressively, for fear the English government would meddle in the colony's business. That business was his business, after all; both Cecil and his father before him had altruistic motives in founding the colony, but they also wanted to make money from it.

Because anti-Catholicism by now was so prevalent in English culture, the Lords Baltimore faced many obstacles to achieving their vision and receiving their profits. In 1649, the colonial assembly passed the Maryland Toleration Act, codifying the Calvert vision and making room for Puritans who had come from Virginia, where attendance at Church of England services was mandatory. The Puritans repaid their welcome by revolting against the Calverts, outlawing both Anglicanism and Catholicism from 1650 to 1658, and burning down all the Catholic churches in Maryland.

Puritans had been disappointed that James I did not wish to fight Catholic Spain or France, but now, when Charles I requested money for a war against Spain, the Puritans opposed him. But the Arminians supported him, and he rewarded them. In 1629, when the Puritans tried to introduce statements condemning Arminianism in Parliament, Charles adjourned that body and decided to rule without it. During the decade of personal rule, he was even more determined to support Laud's efforts for uniformity and against Calvinism.

Charles and Laud tried to force the Church of Scotland, the Presbyterian Kirk, to conform to the doctrines and worship of the Church of England and the *Book of Common Prayer*. When Charles was crowned King at Edinburgh in 1633, the liturgy of coronation, with incense and trumpets, pomp and ceremony, seemed much too Catholic to the Scots. Then Laud introduced the Scottish *Book of Common Prayer*, an anti-Calvinist form of worship, in 1637. A royal proclamation demanded that it become the only form of worship in Scotland and that every parish obtain two copies by Easter of that year. The Scottish bishops tried to suspend the prayer book, but Charles stubbornly ordered them to obey him as king, divinely appointed and ordained.

The Scottish revolt of 1637 had a founding document, the National Covenant, which declared that true Christianity was practiced only in Scotland, under the authority of the Kirk. That

higher authority legitimated disobedience to the King. These conflicts in Scotland led Charles into war, and war led him to seek
money from Parliament, thus ending his personal rule. The spirit of
rebellion then settled upon the more radical Puritans in the English
Parliament. The "Root and Branch" petition of 1640 proposed
wide-ranging reforms, including the end of episcopacy. But the rest
of Parliament did not want to go that far and passed piecemeal
reforms, while at the same time marginalizing the King.

Then in October, 1641 the Catholics in Ireland rose against
Parliament and in support of the King, adding to the conflict. Like
the Presbyterians in the Kirk of Scotland and the Puritans of the
"Root and Branch" party in Parliament in England, the Catholics
of Ireland declared their goals in a document, the Confederation of
Kilkenny. The Irish Catholics—both the native stock and the English who had settled there—united to protect the Catholic Church,
fearing additional Protestant plantations and Parliamentary rule.

Now Charles faced conflict in each of his three kingdoms, England, Scotland, and Ireland. The rebels in Scotland and England
made common cause, while the conflict in Ireland exacerbated their
disagreements with Charles.

The Catholics in Ireland did not proclaim a holy war against
Protestants. Though reports of massacres of English Protestant
plantation owners by Ulster Catholic peasants were tremendously
exaggerated, the Puritans of England looked upon these rebels as
utterly alien and unholy. The House of Commons blamed the Jesuits
for the Catholic uprising, and the City of London demanded an end
to episcopacy with such violence that Commons was forced to
impeach the bishops. Before more violence between the Arminian
High Church hierarchy and the Puritan Parliament could take place,
however, Charles I left London, began to raise his own military
force, and in August 1642, declared war on Parliament.

The Civil War pitted the Royalist Cavaliers against the Puritan
Roundheads. Catholic nobles fought for a king who had never
shown them any great favor simply because he was the enemy of
their enemies, the Puritans.

Charles' Catholic queen traveled to the Netherlands, officially to
accompany Mary, the Princess Royal, to The Hague. Mary was

betrothed to William, Prince of Orange (and would become the mother of William III, whom we will meet in the next chapter). Henrietta Maria also worked to gain support for her husband and to raise funds and purchase supplies.

She returned to England and set up court with Charles in Oxford, using the chapel of Merton College. Because the royal family had fled London, parliamentary Puritans destroyed the furnishings of Henrietta Maria's chapel at Somerset House, shredding the canvas of a Crucifixion painted by Rubens and arresting the Capuchin friars who had served her.[57]

The cathedrals of England, freshly renovated by Archbishop Laud, were special targets of Puritan soldiers. Once they occupied a cathedral town, they proceeded to fulfill an ordinance passed on August 26, 1643 by the House of Commons ordering "the utter demolishing, removing and taking away of all Monuments of Super-stition or Idolatry," including stone altars, candlesticks, crucifixes, pictures, stained glass windows, and any superstitious inscriptions. The ordinance also warned against desecrating tombs, but some-times the soldiers got so carried away destroying things that they forgot that part of it. Here was iconoclasm performed with relish and mockery.

- At Chicester Cathedral, Parliament's troops destroyed the organ, and "dashing the Pipes with their Pole-axes, scoffingly said, 'hark how the Organs go.'"
- They tossed about a chalice at Chicester, while Sir Arthur Haselrig, "dancing and skipping," cried, "There Boys, there Boys, heark, heark, it Rattles, it Rattles."
- At Winchester Cathedral, soldiers and cavalry marched in "with Colours flying, their Drums beating, their Matches fired." They proceeded to destroy the altar, the rail, the *Book of Common Prayer* and choir books, and carvings of Old and New Testament stories, before turning their attention to the tombs and monuments.
- In Exeter, they broke the windows, defaced the bishops' tombs, and broke down the organ, carrying the pipes along with them down the street.

What they could not reach with their swords, pikes or axes, they shot at—wasting ammunition perhaps, but also fulfilling Parliament's ordinance against superstition and idolatry.[58]

Catholic priests in parliamentary territory faced arrest and execution by hanging, drawing, and quartering. One priest, Hugh Green, endured an even more excruciating martyrdom in 1642, when an incompetent barber-cum-executioner tore him apart alive, searching for his heart and cutting out his liver by mistake. After half an hour of agony, the sheriff finally stabbed him to death, and then the godly people of Dorchester played football with his head.[59]

As the hated Catholic Queen who had influenced Charles to leniency toward Catholics and enmity toward Puritans, Henrietta Maria was charged with high treason and impeached by Parliament in 1643. In 1644, after giving birth to a girl, Henrietta Anna, she fled to France, where she lived at St. Germain-en-Laye, the guest of her nephew Louis XIV and his mother and regent Anne of Austria. Her children eventually joined her at the chateau west of Paris where Louis had been born. She continued to work for the Royalist cause and correspond with Charles.

William Laud was tried for treason by Parliament in 1643. The court failed to convict him, so the Long Parliament ordered his execution. Thus, as Owen Chadwick says, they took a step "in the course whereby Englishmen would for years associate the puritan programme with injustice and illegality."[60]

During the Civil War, Parliament replaced the King as the supreme governor of the Church of England, dismantling the hierarchy and condemning the *Book of Common Prayer*. In September of 1643, members of Parliament took the Solemn League and Covenant oath by which they joined in seeking the reform of religion in England and Ireland and the preservation of the true religion in Scotland. They further vowed to pursue "the extirpation of Popery, prelacy (that is, Church government by Archbishops, Bishops, their Chancellors and Commissioners, Deans, Deans and Chapters, Archdeacons, and all other ecclesiastical offices depending on that hierarchy), superstition, heresy, schism, profanes and whatever shall be found contrary to sound doctrine and the power of godliness."[61] What that was, they of course would decide. In addition, Parliament shut down the theaters in London and tried to outlaw the celebration of Christmas as a sign of Catholic superstition.

OLIVER CROMWELL, PARLIAMENT, AND PRESBYTERIAN TRIUMPH

Oliver Cromwell was a Member of Parliament who became the great general of its armies. He was a member of the Independent Party and desired limits on government control of the Church; yet once he came to power, he used his New Model Army to dictate religious observance wherever Parliament gained control. Throughout the Civil War, Parliament set religious policy, advised by the Westminster Assembly of 121 ministers and 30 laymen. It appointed pastors, created committees, and collected pew rentals, while refusing to let the Westminster Assembly enforce discipline and retain those powers for itself.

The unity of the Solemn League and Covenant led to a more Calvinist and Presbyterian church structure and practice. In 1645, the *Book of Common Prayer* was abolished and presbyteries established. Calvinism was now in power in England and the Thirty-Nine Articles were interpreted in Calvinist terms. Once again the government determined official Church worship and doctrine. Bishops, ordained ministers, and deacons were removed and Presbyterian ministers put in their place, and a new wave of iconoclastic destruction swept cathedrals and churches not yet desecrated during the Civil War.

When Charles was defeated and captured, Cromwell pursued the trial and execution of the King. Charles refused to acknowledge the authority of the court in the House of Commons, convened without the House of Lords, comported himself with great dignity at his beheading, and was regarded as a martyr for the Church of England. After his death, a book, the *Eikon Basilike*, was published describing his last hours. It went through 50 editions and spread the belief that the king's execution had been not just a mistake but a sinful murder. (Henrietta Maria never fully recovered from the shock of her husband's execution and wore black for the rest of her life.)

Oliver Cromwell became Lord Protector and found himself in conflict with Parliament just as Charles had. Cromwell called upon the New Model Army to enforce the high standards of personal behavior required by Puritan hatred of vice. Laws were enforced against drunkenness and swearing, but most of all against Christmas. Soldiers entered peoples' homes on Christmas day to confiscate the turkey and pudding. Demanding uncompromising Sunday observance, the Puritans allowed no walking that day except to church services. On Christmas, however, they insisted that shops be open, churches be closed, and people work as usual. If Christmas day happened to fall on a fast day proclaimed by Parliament, the fast took precedence over the feast. The Puritans seemed to fear that joyful Christmas rituals and celebrations would attract people to popery.

In matters of religion, there was more freedom of thought and a wider range of theology, provided it was not Catholic or Episcopalian. Catholics were regarded as traitors and the Mass absolutely forbidden. Anglicans were also seen as disloyal to Cromwell's rule and the *Book of Common Prayer* forbidden— although private devotion was beyond the Puritan's reach, and neither Cromwell nor Parliament ever controlled all of England. Where they were in charge, moreover, people began to tire of this interference in their affairs.

Under Cromwell, too, a committee made up of Presbyterians, Independents (Congregationalists), and Baptists determined who could validly serve as pastors of the Church of England. They also took over the high posts at Oxford and Cambridge. While there was a degree of toleration toward dissent in England, in Ireland Cromwell and his army sought the destruction of Catholicism in retribution for the rebellion of 1641.

CROMWELL IN IRELAND

The deeds of Cromwell and his New Model Army in 1649 during the Irish campaign are infamous. Winston Churchill writes: "Cromwell in Ireland, disposing of overwhelming strength and using it with merciless wickedness, debased the standards of human conduct and sensibly darkened the journey of mankind."[62] For nine months, he led a campaign to destroy the Irish rebels. In violation of the rules of civilized warfare, he allowed and indeed approved the massacre of noncombatants at the sieges of Drogheda and Wexford.

Cromwell called his army's atrocities "the righteous judgment of God upon these barbarous wretches." He believed that the massacres served the good purpose of encouraging other towns and strongholds to surrender without resistance. The tactic worked, as tales of the murder of pregnant women, elderly people, children, priests, and nuns led towns to surrender and sue for peace. When negotiating terms, they would request freedom of religion, but Cromwell would not allow the Mass to be celebrated. Although he could do nothing about anyone's conscience or beliefs, he could interfere with everyone's actions.

Like Elizabeth and James before him, Cromwell used a plantation system to remove Irish Catholic rebels from their land and give it to Protestant soldiers, who either settled down or sold the property. Almost two-thirds of the land of Ireland passed from Catholic ownership. Cromwell also instituted drastic penal laws to restrict Irish Catholic participation in society and government.

Eventually, Cromwell returned to England, even though he would have preferred to stay with the campaign to destroy Catholicism. Able military leader though he was, economic depression, unemployment, and inflation were causing unrest back home.

The New Model Army also had to confront an uprising of the Scots, who had allied with Charles II. The Scots recognized him as King after the death of his father, but he had to agree to Presbyterian Kirk structure—strategic apostasy with which his mother, Henrietta Maria, heartily disagreed. Charles II invaded Scotland in 1650 in an attempt to retake the throne, but the invincible New Model Army defeated his forces and he had to flee again to European exile.

During the Interregnum, meanwhile, the fortunes of the colony in Maryland varied greatly. When Parliament ruled in England, laws against Catholics were in force. Under Cromwell, however, Cecil Calvert, the second Lord Baltimore, was able to reassert his proprietorship. Cromwell took a pragmatic approach to matters of conscience, surprisingly flexible coming from the scourge of Ireland. Calvert regained control of his colony in 1657 and reinstituted his policies of tolerance and religious freedom.

When Cromwell died in 1658, his son Richard briefly succeeded him as Lord Protector. Parliament realized, however, that the Protectorate had only one purpose—power. Richard was deposed because he had no plan or program to address domestic issues. Even a moderate Puritan Parliament was ready for the end of the Interregnum and the experiment in theocracy. The people of England were also ready for the change.

The trio of King, Church of England, and *Book of Common Prayer* became a common cause. Its representative was Charles II, exiled heir of Charles I, the Church of England martyr. Upon the return of the monarchy, Cromwell's body was dug up and he was hung, drawn, and quartered, while many still-living regicides were executed in similar fashion.

At the end of the Interregnum years of Commonwealth and Protectorate, Catholics were a powerless minority in England and an oppressed majority in Ireland. The Restoration and the Cavalier Parliament held no great promise for them. They might have hoped that Charles II's connections with the great Catholic King Louis XIV of France would influence him in their favor, but Charles needed to ally himself with the Church of England in order to reestablish the Stuart dynasty and the monarchy as far as Parliament allowed.

Like the American Civil War, the English Civil War was very costly to infrastructure and population, since the battles were fought at home and the armies were composed of members of divided families. Diane Purkiss tallies the cost:

> Estimates suggest that around 800,000 people in the British Isles died during its course, the majority of them in Ireland. One in four of all men served in the armies on one side or the other, which suggests that a majority of able-bodied men was involved. . . . For years afterwards, the London streets were full of one-legged beggars. Cities and castles were razed to the ground. There were atrocities involving civilians, again especially in Ireland. The war was expensive, and individual families were ruined—or made—by its sweeping hand.[63]

To some, Charles II's return from exile and the restoration of the monarchy meant it had all been for naught. But the rise of Parliament was now assured, and the new King would have to rule with its consent.

CHAPTER

Restoration and Revolution: Charles II and James II, 1660 to 1688

THE RETURN OF ANGLICANISM, 1660 TO 1685

CHARLES II RETURNED TO ENGLAND in 1660 after having lived as an exile in France under the patronage of King Louis XIV. He and his brother James had survived for 16 years in a Catholic, Continental environment. The Restoration meant a near-total reversal of all that Parliament had achieved during the Interregnum. To prepare for it, members of Parliament re-established the power and authority of the monarch, the Episcopal Church of England, and the *Book of Common Prayer.*

New oaths demanded not only loyalty but also nonresistance to the King and his leadership of state and the church. The High Church interpretation of the Thirty-Nine Articles was emphasized. Puritan ministers were removed from their posts as only clergymen ordained by bishops could officiate at religious ceremonies. The Church was Royalist and Parliament was Anglican. Charles' Chancellor, Edward Hyde, Lord Clarendon, sponsored acts of Parliament to suppress the Protestant dissenters, forbidding small groups to convene except under the auspices of the Church of England and barring ministers from coming within five miles of parishes from which they had been removed.

As Winston Churchill notes, in contrast to the Elizabethan settlement the Restoration settlement did not seek unity and uniformity in compromise. The Cavalier Parliament simply established the Anglican sect as power base of government and church, forcing out those who disagreed with them.[64]

The Restoration also benefited the Maryland colony, which experienced its most prosperous period during Charles II's 25-year reign. Cecil Calvert's son Charles served as governor in Maryland until his father's death in 1675. Cecil, second Lord Baltimore had, in John D. Krugler's words, "been singularly important. . . . With remarkable persistence, he had kept the enterprise going. Catholic Maryland had been his Maryland."[65]

Charles II brought Catholicism back to the English court by marrying a Catholic princess, Catherine of Braganza. There were priests in her household and Mass was celebrated in the same chapel at St. James that Charles I had built first for the Infanta of Spain and then for Henrietta Maria of France. The Queen Mother returned to England briefly, then returned to France, where she died. She was buried in St. Denis (her tomb was desecrated during the French Revolution). One can only imagine what she must have felt at seeing the banquet room from which her husband had walked to his beheading and her chapel, so wrecked and destroyed.

Charles was a crypto-Catholic, yet lived profligately. He had several mistresses, both Catholic and Protestant—once, when facing an angry mob, Nell Gwynne referred to herself as "the Protestant whore." Yet the moral laxity of his court did not provoke a storm of outrage among the Anglican clergy, who were afraid of being thought too Puritanical. Charles did have a favorite illegitimate son, James Croft Scott, the Duke of Monmouth, who became a rival for the throne to Charles' brother James.

At first, Charles was very popular. The arts, music, and theater were restored to English culture. The King's heroic image made him a model, like his idol and sometime ally, Louis XIV of France. Others at court adopted his style and his morals, until his sexual behavior became too rapacious to tolerate.

The Restoration era in literature is commonly known as the Age of Dryden, since John Dryden (1631–1700), a convert to Catholicism, dominated the literary scene. As poet, critic, and playwright, Dryden excelled in satire, panegyric, tragedy, comedy, epic, and religious poetry. Dryden attended Oliver Cromwell's funeral in November 1658, marching in procession with Andrew Marvell and John Milton. He even wrote a poem in somewhat restrained praise of Cromwell. But when Charles II returned, he marked the event with a much more effusively celebratory poem and began his career as a public poet in the Royalist cause. His poem "Absalom and Achitophel" tells the story of the Exclusionist crisis, when the Earl of Shaftesbury (Achitophel) sought to use Monmouth (Absalom) to replace James in the succession. In 1687 he published *The Panther and the Hind* to celebrate his conversion to Roman Catholicism. But James II was deposed in 1688, and in short order Dryden was replaced as Poet Laureate and left public office. He spent the last two years of his life translating classic Greek and Latin works. Dryden died in 1700 and is buried in Westminster Abbey.

In 1668 or 1669, James, the Duke of York, secretly converted to Catholicism. Married to Anne Hyde, the Earl of Clarendon's daughter, he had two daughters, Mary and Anne, and served as Lord Admiral of the English Navy. Charles was furious with him and demanded that Mary and Anne be raised Protestant. Parliament feared that since Charles and Catherine had no legitimate children, James, a Catholic, would succeed his brother. When the Earl of Shaftesbury introduced and Parliament passed the Test Act requiring office-holders to swear an oath denying Transubstantiation and receive Anglican communion, James refused to swear and resigned his commission. Having herself become a Catholic, Anne Hyde died in 1671, after which Charles allowed James to marry again, at the suggestion of Louis XIV, an Italian Catholic princess, Mary Beatrice of Modena.

Charles himself continued to flirt with Catholicism, negotiating a treaty with Louis XIV in a war against the Protestant Dutch. He even promised, secretly, that he would become a Roman Catholic. (Of course, he had promised the Scots in 1650 that he would become a Presbyterian.) In 1672, he proclaimed a Declaration of Indulgence to allow Catholic and Protestant dissenters to worship freely in private. But Parliament opposed the measure, and Charles had to withdraw the bill.

There were several reasons why Roman Catholics were still so hated and feared in seventeenth-century England. The balance of power in Europe was one, as J. P. Kenyon describes in his study, *The Popish Plot.*

> The confidently expected victory of Truth over Falsehood had somehow never occurred, and the European rivalry between Catholicism and Protestantism had dragged on into the seventeenth century, with the Catholics steadily gaining ground; first the southern Netherlands had been lost, then southern Germany, and in 1648, when the Thirty Year's War ended, Protestantism had been driven out to the periphery of Europe, where it was precariously lodged in North Germany, Holland, Scandinavia, England, and Scotland; all with the exception of Holland poor, thinly populated second-class nations.

Yet, after defeating the Spanish Armada, the English were confident that no invasion could succeed and mainly feared conspiracies from within. They looked at Catholics, and especially the Jesuits, as instigators, based on the lingering legacy of the Gunpowder Plot of 1605. The English were sure that if Catholics seized control, Protestants would burn, as they had in Smithfield's pyres in the days of "Bloody Mary."

"The obstinate durability of the Catholic community," in spite of years of penal laws, also frustrated English Protestants. "Although by the death of Elizabeth I in 1603 it was clearly a minority of the population, it never proved possible to eliminate it entirely, as corresponding Protestant minorities had been eliminated in Spain and Italy, and were to be eliminated in France after 1685, with almost complete success." This failure to obliterate the Catholic minority in England was magnified by the endurance of the Catholic majority in Ireland.

Finally, as Kenyon notes, English Protestants were never completely sure of the Stuart dynasty's loyalty to Protestantism. James I's attempts to convene an ecumenical council with the Pope and to marry his heir to the Infanta of Spain, Charles I's marriage to a Catholic Princess, Laud's Anglo-Catholic Church policies, the current King's crypto-Catholicism, and his brother and heir's conversion to Catholicism—all these factors made the Stuarts suspect.[66]

Even before the Popish Plot sparked these anti-Catholic embers, the Great Fire of 1666 fanned the fears of Catholic conspiracies against England. Destroying many churches and buildings in the City of London, including Old St. Paul's, the blaze was blamed on Catholics, though with little evidence. Christopher Wren rebuilt St. Paul's and built the Monument, commemorating the conflagration. In 1681 an inscription was added to the Monument declaring that, "Popish frenzy, which wrought such horrors, is not yet quenched." These words were not removed until 1831. After the failure of his Declaration of Indulgence and the passage of the Test Act, Charles' foreign policy swung against the Catholic Louis XIV and toward the Protestant William of Orange. Mary, James' first daughter, was married in 1677 to the great Protestant hero (who was, after all, James' nephew). At the urging of the new Chancellor, Thomas Osborne, Earl of Danby, enforcement of the penal laws became more severe.

The Church of England had been reestablished, Puritans were no longer a factor, and Catholics were still being persecuted, yet in its advocates' eyes Anglicanism was not as strong as it should have been. In reaction to the Puritan attempts of the past sixteen years, there was no desire to reform or correct any abuses in the Church. The rejection of Puritanism meant that even elementary moral standards were weakened—as witness the profligacy of Charles' court, his many noble married mistresses, and his illegitimate children.

Ordered liturgical worship returned and the beauty of the churches was restored. Purcell wrote great liturgical music, and Christopher Wren and Nicholas Hawksmoor designed great houses of worship. Nevertheless, the established Church's hold on people's minds and hearts was weakened, with the rational and scientific spirit of the age, influenced by Francis Bacon's *Novum Organum* (1620), fostering a division between faith and reason. The Anglican Church could not return to the days of William Laud, and no one had the power he had once held to enforce its doctrinal and moral teachings.

THE POPISH PLOT, 1678 TO 1679

The fear that Catholics had inspired in the days of the Armada or the Gunpowder Plot revived during Charles II's reign. In 1678, a shyster named Titus Oates presented evidence of a Catholic plot to assassinate the King. There was no plot, and Charles knew that Oates was a liar, but he was unable to convince the anti-Catholic Parliament to be reasonable. Parliament passed a second Test Act to exclude all Catholics from court, and Charles had to send James and his wife into temporary exile to protect them. Innocent Jesuits, secular priests, and laymen were accused and executed, simply for being Catholics. Oliver Plunkett, the Bishop of Armagh in Ireland, was brought to England to be tried where he could present no witnesses or defense. Found guilty of treason on July 1, 1681, he became the last Catholic priest to be hung, drawn, and quartered at Tyburn. He was canonized by Pope Paul VI in 1975.

In 1681 Titus Oates was tried and convicted of perjury—but like a modern newspaper correction, it was not headline news that Catholics were not plotting against the King, and Parliament would not admit having committed any injustice in accepting Oates' perjured testimony. This episode, like the Great Fire, shows how deeply anti-Catholicism had sunk into the English mentality. Charles II did not have the power and influence one might have expected from the Restoration settlement, and his own fascination with Roman Catholicism made his advisors and government nervous.

The prospect of a truly Catholic king loomed before Parliament as Charles II's reign ended after 25 years without a legitimate Protestant heir. One party wanted to exclude James, Duke of York, because he was Catholic, and supported the succession of James, Duke of Monmouth, one of Charles' illegitimate children, because he was a Protestant. The other party was deeply committed to a legitimate succession and to their oath of nonresistance to the King, who had named his brother as his heir. The opposing sides gave each other insulting nicknames: the Exclusionists were called Whigs, or covenanting Scots cattle thieves; those supporting orderly succession were called Tories, or papist Irish thugs. The Tories supported James even though they were not sure how a Catholic could rule a Protestant nation and be head of the Church of England. But they were certain they did not want a return of the Commonwealth, and they prevailed, dominating the court and government from the last years of Charles' reign to James II's reign.

JAMES II AND VII, 1685 TO 1688

Charles was received into the Catholic Church on his deathbed in 1685 by the priest who had helped him escape from Scotland in 1650. His brother and his wife both were instrumental in his final conversion. Clearing the room of anyone who was not Catholic, James led Father John Huddleston to Charles's deathbed where Charles made his confession, was absolved, and received his First Holy Communion as a Roman Catholic. When Thomas Ken, Bishop of Bath and Wells, entered the room, he began to press Charles to receive the sacraments of the Church of England. Charles refused.

Now James ascended to the throne. It was almost a relief to have as king someone forthright and honest about his faith. At the beginning of his reign, James made it clear that he knew he needed the support of the Church of England to rule England well. He also wanted to work with the Church to relieve restrictions on Catholics. He certainly needed Parliament to raise an army against the Protestant, illegitimate son of Charles II, the Duke of Monmouth, who attempted to invade England. The ruling classes and people were behind James II at first, and supported him in the struggles with Monmouth, even though having a Catholic king in a Protestant country caused some tension. The story is told that as James was going to Mass and was about to enter the chapel, the English courtier escorting him stopped at the door. "Your father would have gone farther," James remonstrated. The noble replied, "Your father would not have gone so far."

Historians and biographers have often commented on the mystery of James' conversion to Catholicism. Perhaps the years of exile in Catholic France influenced him. Until he became king, he exhibited no leadership among Catholics in England; but once crowned, he launched on a course that led once again to revolution, albeit less violent and disruptive to the nation at large. The Glorious Revolution, as

Protestant Whig historians have dubbed it, centered on the issue of the relationship between the King and the ruling upper class on matters of church and state. Finding the country socially tranquil and economically prosperous, James began to take steps that infuriated the Anglican Parliament and Church and led to his downfall.

He began by trying to exempt Catholic army officers from the Test Act. James had packed the army with Catholics while fighting off invasion by the Duke of Monmouth, and now he told Parliament it was unfair to reward their good service with dishonor. Then he moved to re-establish relations with the Vatican, requesting appointment of a Vicar Apostolate and beginning discussions on the establishment of new dioceses, with new Catholic bishops. He helped found a Catholic press, invited priests and monks to the Court of St. James, and assisted with the founding of small religious houses and a Jesuit school, where some Protestant parents enrolled their children to take advantage of the excellent education offered there.

James worked to prepare the parliamentary elections of 1687 in hopes of repealing the Test Act and Penal Laws, thereby freeing both Roman Catholic and Protestant dissenters to worship and live their faith. He thought the dissenting Protestants would support him, since he proposed greater religious freedom than anywhere in Europe. Their fear of Catholics and bias them were too strong, especially as James continued to support Catholics so publicly. At Oxford University, for instance, he promoted Catholics to high positions at Christ Church and University Colleges and appointed Catholic fellows at Magdalene College.

Winston Churchill remarks that we will never know what James ultimately intended. If it was to grant Catholics and Protestant dissenters freedom of worship and stop at that, he deserves recognition as a great modern hero. If it was to use toleration as a stepping-stone in making Catholicism the state religion in place of the Church of England, he was a dangerous despot. In any event, the ruling classes, both Tories and Whigs, along with William and Mary of Orange, stopped him before he could carry his plan—whatever it was—through to completion.[67]

Two events in 1687 brought James' efforts to improve the position of Catholics in England to a head. First came the announcement that James' Catholic wife was pregnant. Both Whigs and Tories began to fear she might have a son, who would displace James' Protestant daughters in the line of succession. Then, as head of the Church of England, James ordered the bishops to read from the pulpit the Declaration of Indulgence declaring religious freedom. Seven High Church bishops refused, including William Sancroft, the Archbishop of Canterbury, and Thomas Ken, Bishop of Bath and Wells. James had them arrested, taken to the Tower, and tried for seditious libel. Their acquittal signaled the defeat of his religious policy.

Then in 1688, James Francis Edward was born. It was rumored that the pregnancy had been a deception and a baby was smuggled into the bedroom in a warming pan—rumors that Princess Anne abetted and urged upon her sister Mary in Holland. But the evident arrival on the scene of a Catholic Prince of Wales and heir to the throne was a serious matter. Leaders of Parliament and the Church of England saw a real possibility, even probability, that Catholicism would be reestablished in England and would perhaps become the national religion. Both Whigs and Tories—including the bishops whom James had arrested—were convinced that the foundations of religious and political life in England were jeopardized by the rule of James II and the succession of James III.

Violating their oaths of nonresistance and their commitment to orderly succession, members of Parliament asked William of Orange and Mary to come to England. When William invaded England, on November 5, 1688, James found himself without the support of the army, as the Protestant officers fled. King James left England with his second family, while his first family—his ungrateful daughters, as he called them—invaded. Anne left her father and joined William and Mary to reassert the Protestant Stuart succession. The Tory party reluctantly accepted the Whig view that James had abdicated by leaving England and taking refuge in France. William of Orange was heralded not as king but as the Protestant champion who would save England from Roman Catholicism. That he came on the fifth of November, anniversary of the Gunpowder Plot, and a hundred years after the Spanish Armada, only emphasized that role.

Parliament arranged the settlement of the Glorious Revolution, determining who would rule and how and deciding the relationship between the Church of England and the constitutional monarchy. Some of the stipulations of the acts of settlement posed immediate problems. The Test Act now applied to the monarch, but William of Orange was a Dutch Protestant who did not receive communion in the Church of England—though he had no problem denying the Catholic doctrine of Transubstantiation. Parliament suggested that Mary reign alone as Queen, but William would not accept the position of consort. So it was decided that they would reign together; at least one monarch passed the Test.

Shocked that William of Orange would become King and governor of the Church of England, some of the bishops who had opposed James refused to swear the oath to William. These non-juring bishops, as they were known, were removed from their sees. Among them were William Sancroft and Thomas Ken, one of the great hymn writers of the Church of England, who authored "Praise God, from Whom All Blessings Flow."

Parliamentary acts made sure that a Roman Catholic would never come near the throne of England again. No king or queen could be a Catholic or marry a Catholic. No Catholic could be regent, Lord Lieutenant of Ireland, or Prime Minister. The Glorious Revolution of 1688 guaranteed that Roman Catholics would have no power in the government of England for centuries to come.

The fall of James II also meant the end of the great experiment in religious freedom and tolerance in Maryland. Charles Calvert, the third Lord Baltimore, was not the leader and diplomat his father had been. Born and raised a Roman Catholic unlike his father and grandfather, he may, as John D. Krugler notes, have been too complacent about Catholic success in Maryland.[68]

Under the Calvert model of church-state relations, Catholics, Quakers, and Protestant dissenters had built their own schools and chapels and thrived. The Episcopalians, however, did not fare so well. Dependent on government to provide them with structures and hierarchy, they did not have "the missionary zeal of the Quakers and the affluence of the Catholics," so they "saw their only hope in a tax-supported institution."[69]

In 1689, the Calverts were overthrown by a Protestant uprising. William and Mary's government ratified the coup, took control of the colony, and established religious uniformity under the Church of England. The great experiment in tolerance and freedom of religion—and in an early form of separation of church and state—was over; but it would influence the Constitution of the United States. Charles Calvert, third Lord Baltimore, died in exile from Maryland in 1715. The fourth Lord Baltimore, Benedict Leonard, converted to Anglicanism in order to regain the proprietorship of the colony.

The two Stuart heirs of Charles I had come to the throne hoping to restore the power structures as they were before the Civil War and the execution of their father. Parliament and the ruling classes seemed ready to work with them at the beginning of their respective reigns, but Charles II's flirtation with Catholicism and James II's conversion unsettled the foundations of the Restoration. The uncertain compromise of the Church of England could no longer uphold the legitimate succession of the monarchy. Starting with the Glorious Restoration and continuing through the eighteenth and the nineteenth centuries, the alliance of church and state was a fractured façade.

Yet the Restoration of the Stuarts gave Catholics some hope for a while. Charles II's Catholic Queen had priests at court, celebrating Mass in the chapel built for Henrietta Maria. If the Catholics had known that Charles had promised Louis XIV to become Catholic himself, they would have rejoiced. As it was, they knew that he wanted to extend toleration to them, but that Parliament prevented him. In time, however, the best opportunity for Catholicism in England since Mary I failed miserably. Catholics, for whom a doorway had seemed to be opening, were completely shut out from power and influence. Parliament had exerted its majestic will to arrange the succession, as it would again in 1701, and limit toleration to Protestant dissidents. Catholics would have to wait another century and a half for legal toleration.

9

CHAPTER

The Aftermath
of the Glorious Revolution
in the Eighteenth Century

INTRODUCTION TO THE EIGHTEENTH CENTURY
AND THE HOUSE OF HANOVER

SOON, THE STUARTS FACED THE ULTIMATE CRISIS: the end of their dynasty. Mary had died in 1694, and William reigned without her. Princess Anne, William and Mary's heir apparent, had been pregnant 18 times, but William, Duke of Gloucester, was the only child to survive infancy. He died at age 11 on July 29, 1700.

Parliament decided the issue, passing the Act of Settlement in 1701. It passed over all the closer Catholic candidates, especially James II's son, James Francis Edward Stuart, to find a Protestant heir to the throne, although not necessarily Anglican. Sophia, Electress of Hanover, was Parliament's choice. Youngest daughter of Frederick V, erstwhile King of Bohemia, and Elizabeth Stuart, she was James I's granddaughter, as Charles II and James II had been his grandsons.

Princess Anne knew Parliament's decision was unjust. It was she, after all, who had abetted the rumor of the warming pan when James Francis Edward was born. But she went along with the Act of Settlement when she succeeded to the throne upon William III's death in 1702. She was a successful and popular monarch, although by then Parliament and her ministers largely ran the country. Those who enjoy irony should reflect on the fact that the English Reformation had begun with Henry VIII's fear that his only legitimate heir would be female, yet among the most successful English monarchs are four women: Elizabeth I, Anne, Victoria, and Elizabeth II. John Knox's "monstrous reign of women" turned out not so monstrous after all.

Nevertheless, Anne still influenced government affairs by her choice of ministers and favorites. Whigs and the Tories fought for control of the government. Because the Tories favored the Church of England, Anne personally favored them. Because the Whigs supported England's role in the War of Spanish Succession (an attempt to prevent the union of Spain and France under one crown), Anne had to work with them, however reluctantly. In religious matters, the Whigs either favored Protestant dissenters or took a Deist approach.

When a Tory government in 1710 sought peace at the end of the War of Spanish Succession, the Whigs opposed the Treaty of Utrecht. The Tories had a majority in the House of Commons, but lacked one in the House of Lords. Anne thereupon packed Lords with twelve new Tory peers, thus giving the party the majority it needed to accept the treaty and end the war. Thereafter she reigned with a Tory government in place until her death in 1714.

Just before Anne died, so did Sophia, the Electress of Hanover, and her right of succession to the English throne passed to her son George, Elector of Hanover. At this juncture, however, some Tories proved very uncomfortable with their earlier choices to depose James II in favor of William of Orange and Mary (1688) and deny James Frances Edward Stuart his rightful inheritance (1701). They supported the Jacobite cause in 1715, and after its defeat (to be covered later in this chapter) were forced out of power, while the Church of England lost power and influence together with them.

THE ENLIGHTENMENT CHURCH OF ENGLAND

The Glorious Revolution had weakened the Church of England's Via Media image. The link between church and king was broken, as Parliament and Convocation led the Church. The Tory wing of the Church was forced out first by the Oath of Allegiance to William and Mary in 1688 and then by the succession of George I. Now there were two groups of non-juring bishops and ministers.

Parliament in 1689 had passed an Act of Toleration for Dissenting [Protestant] Congregations. In essence, this was an admission that the Church of England was no longer the one, true church in England. Except that Catholics were not included, it provided the same kind of toleration that James II had proposed. The Church of England had no control over who would be tolerated, since the religious test consisted of an oath of loyalty to the Crown, not to any confession of faith, and involved no examination of doctrine or sacramental initiation.

Latitudinarian Whigs felt that matters of doctrine, liturgical practice, and ecclesiastical organization were of relatively little importance. But the issue of religion and the status of the Church of England made it possible for the Tories to take power in 1709. Henry Sacheverell, a Tory clergyman, preached two sermons critical of the Whig regime and became a Tory hero when the government prosecuted him for seditious libel. When the court suspended Sacheverell for three years and demanded that his two sermons be burned, it was a de facto defeat for the Whigs reminiscent of James II's prosecution of the Archbishop of Canterbury and other bishops who refused to read the Declaration of Indulgence. The Whigs had gone too far. The next election brought the Tories to power in a landslide. Queen Anne was pleased at the Whig defeat and happy to have the Tories in control to support the Church of England.

From the Glorious Revolution throughout the eighteenth century, the Tory party was in a precarious position. Even when the Tories held power, they were denying their principles. The party of legitimate succession had helped interfere with and rearrange the succession twice, denying the rightful heir the throne because he was Catholic. The party of the Church of England cooperated with an Act of Toleration that reduced the power of Anglicanism. The Party of order and nonresistance supported the Jacobite cause against the legally constituted monarch. Yet, the Tories truly hoped that the Catholic Pretender would return to England. He called himself James III and lived in exile, supported by Louis XIV at St. Germain-en-Laye.

As king, George I favored the Whig party and removed all Tories and High Churchmen from both the administration and the episcopacy. After all, some of these—notably Francis Atterbury, the Archbishop of Rochester (St. John Fisher's see), and Henry St. John, Viscount Bolingbroke—had worked against his claim to the throne. He also dismissed the Convocation of Bishops, effectively leaving the Church of England without leadership. George I was more interested in Hanoverian issues in Germany than in English policy and was very unpopular. Having the law, the military, and the Whig party on his side, he did not care.

The Whig monarchy and state-mandated toleration contributed to the weakness of the Church of England, but the rise of Deism and atheism during the Enlightenment contributed even more. In 1695 John Locke published his *Essay on the Reasonableness of Christianity*. The following year brought John Toland's *Christianity Not Mysterious*, with its daunting subtitle: "A Treatise Showing that There is Nothing in the Gospel Contrary to Reason; Not Above It; and That No Christian Doctrine Can Be Properly Called a Mystery." Reason became the central reality and guide. Reason and faith were considered to be completely separate, while God's revelation was thought of as a kind of supplement to what reason could discover without faith.

Under the influence of Locke and Toland, heirs of the Cambridge Platonists of the seventeenth century, mystery was effectively banished from religious life. Wonder was eliminated, the supernatural curtailed, and any suggestion of priestly or sacramental action was dismissed out of hand. The denial of the supernatural led to an equivocal view of the Holy Bible that rejected the miraculous and the supernatural. This spirit of mistrust of the miraculous moved Thomas Jefferson to edit the four gospels, omitting miracles and including only the moral teachings of Jesus Christ.

In this high noon of latitudinarianism, reason and moderation were the norm. Alexander Pope sums up their effects on religion in the *Essay on Man*:

> Know then thyself, presume not God to scan;
> The proper study of mankind is man.[70]

Pope was born and raised a Catholic and educated at secret Catholic schools, but as much as anyone he gave voice to the spirit of his rationalistic, deistic age.

Bishops and other clergy exhibited a theological vagueness, with views on doctrine so nebulous that it was hard to say whether they were heretical or orthodox. Churchmen emphasized moral duty and ethical standards, but even here the message was moderation and reasonableness, magnanimity and the mean. Jane Austen shows this mindset at work in the opening sequences of *Sense and Sensibility*. Having promised his father on his deathbed to look after his stepmother and stepsisters, John Dashwood determines to give them £3,000. Fanny, his wife, objects that they surely do not expect so much, and Dashwood reduces the gift to £1,500. Fanny continues to demur, and he proposes an annuity of £100. But she reasonably points out that this way he could end up giving much more than £1,500. His stepmother and stepsisters don't really need servants, horses, society, or fancy housekeeping, she insists. So Dashwood's generosity turns out to be occasional gifts of £50. John and Fanny ignore the real needs of the Dashwood sisters, dowries for their marriages, and a social life that will let them meet eligible men. Fanny has argued her husband out of doing what he promised his father, all with reason and moderation.

Religion became a matter of behaving well, not praying well or believing well. Under the control of the state, the Church of England did not build new churches to accommodate shifting populations nor did it repair the existing ones. Congregations wanted to hear sermons, and "when they were not provided, the people would not attend."[71] The Church of England's latitudinarian moderation could satisfy the mind but it could not reach the heart.

There were attempts at reviving the Church of England in the eighteenth century. One of the second group of non-jurors—those who would not swear the oath of allegiance to George I—was William Law. His book *The Call to the Serious and Devout Life* met peoples' need for a religious faith that engaged the heart as well as the head, the emotions and will as much as reason, and made some demands for self-sacrifice and devotion. But perhaps the greatest revival came through the Methodist movement. John Wesley and his evangelical friend George Whitefield touched hearers' hearts with sermons preached to vast crowds out of doors (because they were not welcome in Anglican churches), often in dramatic dusk or dawn settings.

Wesley had begun to evangelize at Oxford University, where he and a group of fellow scholars gathered in his "Holy Club" for Bible study, to develop discipline, and to care for the poor. They were mocked for their enthusiasm. Aidan Nichols says the Wesleyans "were moving on similar lines to those which the Tractarian movement would rediscover a hundred years later"—a stress on practical good works, high-church liturgy, devotion to the Fathers, and strict asceticism.[72]

After a trip to the colony of Georgia and disappointment in missionary work, Wesley returned to England. Wherever he spoke, he left behind an organization to lead his followers in Bible study, discipline, and caring for the poor—the method he had developed at Oxford—thus sustaining revival.

Wesley and Whitefield eventually parted ways because they disagreed on free will and predestination. Like the great Caroline divines, Wesley was an Arminian—a believer in free will, that is—while Whitefield was a Calvinist; but the two men strove for personal holiness. One of Wesley's favorite books was *The Imitation of Christ*. The spirituality of the Methodist movement is also expressed in the hymns that Charles Wesley wrote, among them "Christ the Lord is Risen Today," "Come, Holy Ghost, Our Hearts Inspire," "O For a Thousand Tongues to Praise," "Come, Thou Long-Expected Jesus," "Rejoice, the Lord is King." Roman Catholics sing these Wesley hymns today at Holy Mass. They convey great devotion and love of Jesus Christ and certainty in his grace and mercy, along with feelings of unworthiness due to personal sin and weakness.

Wesley never meant to found a new church. He intended to revive the Church of England from within. But Methodism did eventually break away from the Church of England, because the established church would not ordain Methodists. The Evangelical movement stayed firmly within the Church of England, and in the nineteenth century under the leadership of William Wilberforce, would contribute to the end of slavery in the British Empire. Three of Wilberforce's sons, Henry, Robert Isaac, and William, became Catholic in the nineteenth century, to the shock of their congregations and friends.

THE JACOBITE CAUSE AND CATHOLIC NADIR

The eighteenth century was the low point for Catholics in England, even lower than the periods of greatest persecution under Elizabeth and James. Catholics suffered from political weakness and social ostracism. They were not persecuted, because the official Church did not really care about doctrine or worship, so that there were no martyrs to encourage the faithful. As Lucy Beckett summarizes: "The eighteenth century, caring less than the seventeenth about every Christian issue, including the truths of revelation, on the whole merely ignored Catholics, so long—and this is very England—as they behaved as coolly about their religion as everyone else was expected to behave about his."[73] Although the government did not strictly enforce the penal laws (unless one of the Hanoverians needed extra cash and decided to tax Catholics further), social isolation, political impotence, and dwindling numbers contributed to making this century a dismal time for English Catholics.

The Catholic Bogeyman could still inspire fear in the populace, however, mainly because Catholics were suspected of Jacobitism as supporters of the claims of James III, Bonnie Prince Charlie, or other Catholic Stuart descendants. Although both Tory and Whig leadership in England had asked William and Mary to come to England and settled upon them as joint rulers, they faced considerable opposition in Scotland and Ireland. In 1689, John Graham of Claverhouse, First Viscount of Dundee ("Bonnie Dundee") organized an army of Scottish clans which defeated William's army at the Battle of Killiecrankie on July 27 that year. Unfortunately for James' cause, however, Bonnie Dundee himself was mortally wounded. Then the Jacobites were defeated within less than a month by Covenanting supporters of William and Mary at the Battle of Dunkeld on August 12. After the defeat of the Jacobites in Scotland, the battle for James' crown continued in Ireland. James lost the Battle of the Boyne, when he faced his son-in-law on July 12, 1690, and spent the rest of his life in France. Even today Protestant Orangemen (taking their name from William of Orange) commemorate the Battle of the Boyne every July 12 with provocative parades through Catholic neighborhoods in Northern Ireland.

In the aftermath of this Jacobite uprising, William offered a pardon to the Highland clans of Scotland, setting a deadline in the middle of winter. After the brutal Massacre of Glencoe on February 13, 1692, when members of the Campbell clan, supporters of William, killed members of the MacDonald clan, other reluctant Jacobites fell in line and swore the oath of allegiance to William and Mary. But the scandal of the massacre, with women and children of the MacDonald clan dying of exposure after their homes were burned down, was a blow to William's reputation, especially since he was slow to punish the wrongdoers.

In Ireland, William continued the Tudor and Stuart policy of taking land from the native Irish and giving it to those who supported his rule. Although the Treaty of Limerick in 1691 was initially a fair settlement, drastic penal laws were passed in 1695. Many Irish went to France to serve in Irish Brigades, and fought in later Jacobite uprisings in 1715 and 1745, led by James' son and grandson.

James II, the Old Pretender, went into exile, hosted by King Louis XIV at St. Germain-en-Laye, west of Paris, where he held court with Mary Beatrice, surrounded by Jacobite supporters. Their daughter, Louise Marie, was born in exile in 1692.

When James II died in 1701, his son James III became the Young Pretender. In 1715 he led an uprising in Scotland. It was perhaps the best opportunity for the Catholic Stuarts, since many in England and Scotland (Ireland was too crushed after the Battle of the Boyne to be involved) were dissatisfied with George I, especially after the financial ruin of the South Sea Bubble. Nevertheless, the Hanoverian forces near Perth overwhelmed the Jacobite army, and James III fled. Once the French court acknowledged the Hanoverian succession, it could not provide either refuge or funds, so James III wandered in Europe before settling in Rome under papal protection.

His sons, Charles Edward and Henry Benedict, were called the Prince of Wales and the Duke of York. With lukewarm support from Louis XV, Charles Edward, nicknamed Bonnie Prince Charlie, led the next attempt at invasion in 1745. After winning at Prestonpans— and even holding court at Holyroodhouse Palace in Edinburgh—and victory at Falkirk, with a brief foray into England, Charles and his

Jacobite forces were defeated by the Duke of Cumberland at Culloden on April 15, 1746. With the help of Flora McDonald and other Jacobite supporters, Bonnie Prince Charlie eluded capture for a year in the Highlands and finally returned to the Continent.

His younger brother Henry became a priest and Cardinal in Rome. In Charles' eyes, this was a betrayal of the Stuart cause, for which he continued to fight. While his father and brother remained in Rome, Charles wandered about Europe trying to raise support for one more invasion. He even visited London and briefly became an Anglican in an attempt to gain support for his cause. After the death of James III on January 1, 1766, Charles came to Rome, but he was disappointed that Pope Clement XIII refused to acknowledge him as Charles III, King of England, Ireland, and Scotland.

Upon his death on January 30, 1788 (the same date as Charles I's execution), his brother Cardinal Stuart halfheartedly declared himself Henry IX. After Napoleon's terms of indemnity in Rome and exile to Venice left the Cardinal King destitute, King George III granted him £4,000 a year. Once Napoleon fell, Henry returned to Rome and died there on July 13, 1807, the last direct descendant in the Stuart line. The Prince Regent, later King George IV, paid for the monument in St. Peter's Basilica, with its inscription (in Latin):

James III,
Son of King James II of Great Britain
Charles Edward and Henry, Dean of the Cardinal Fathers
Sons of James III
The Last of the Royal House of Stuart

While the Stuart Pretenders were Kings over the Water, toasted by Jacobites in England, Scotland, and Ireland, those who helped them were arrested, imprisoned, fined, and even executed. Each time an exiled Stuart led a failed military invasion, the English forces followed his path of retreat in Ireland and Scotland, killing the wounded and pillaging the villages. The Duke of Cumberland was nicknamed the Butcher of Culloden for the viciousness of the aftermath of that battle. Culloden also brought the banning of kilt and tartan and the destruction of the clan system in Scotland.

During this low point in the history of English Catholicism the Vicar Apostolic was Bishop Richard Challoner. Born in 1691 to Presbyterian parents, he became a Catholic as a boy and went to Douai to study for the priesthood. After several years an as administrator, he returned to England in 1730 as a missionary priest. He was coadjutor bishop for the Vicar Apostolic of London from 1741 to 1758, when he succeeded to that office in which he served from 1758 to 1781. Challoner was the most prominent English Catholic leader of his time, barely escaping the wrath of the Gordon Riots in 1778.

In the midst of his pastoral duties, Challoner produced a library of books for the Catholics of England. These include an updated and corrected version of the Douai Bible, devotional manuals, translations of medieval spiritual writers, polemical works defending Catholicism, religious education materials, and works on Church history, especially the early history of Christianity in England.

With Catholics a fragmented, isolated, mistrusted minority, Challoner's works provided a focal point that reminded them of their heritage. Challoner recalled to this fellow Catholics the heroic martyrs of the sixteenth century, Campion and Clitherow, Southwell and Walpole, and reminded them of the heritage of the Venerable Bede, St. Aidan, and St. Augustine of Canterbury. He embodied Catholic perseverance in difficult times.

If there was something un-English and disloyal about being a Catholic in England, to be a Catholic in Ireland was even worse. Catholics were still the majority there, since not even Cromwell's victories and expanded plantation policies could change Irish Catholic culture. Still, as Edmund Burke pointed out, the penal laws in Ireland were well suited for the oppression, impoverishment, degradation, and debasement of these people. Although the penal laws clearly targeted Irish Roman Catholics, the mentality of the government was that "the law does not presume any such person to exist as an Irish Roman Catholic."

- Catholic education was illegal. In order to teach the catechism, the Gaelic language, and Irish history, priests taught in "hedgerow" schools, with lookouts posted. It was also illegal for Catholics to send their children abroad under the Education Act of 1695.

- It was illegal for a Catholic bishop to be present in Ireland. The usual penalty for treason remained hanging, drawing, and quartering (the Banishment Act, 1697).

- Property laws were designed to keep Irish Roman Catholics from owning land. They could not buy or lease it, and those who owned any could not bequeath it to just one heir but had to break it up among all of them. The property laws also favored conversion to the Anglican Church of Ireland, as the convert received property and wealth. If, for example, a Catholic wife became Protestant, she would have all the property rights and custody of the children (the Popery Act, 1704).

- The Registration Act of 1704 allowed a Catholic priest to serve in a designated county, providing he paid a £50 good behavior bond and remained there. If he became a priest of the Anglican Church of Ireland, he would receive a £20 stipend, to be paid by his former Catholic parishioners.

Although Catholics were still the majority in Ireland, they were not allowed to rule themselves. They were able to vote, but no Catholic could be elected to office because of the Test Act and the Oath of Allegiance.

Toward the end of the eighteenth century there was some relief for Catholics in England. But the mitigating laws met with opposition. In 1778, when Parliament passed the Catholic Relief Act enabling Catholics to inherit and purchase land, there were anti-Catholic demonstrations and violence in London and Edinburgh. These Gordon Riots, as they were called, were blamed on the inflammatory rhetoric of Lord Gordon.

Yet the sufferings of exiled French Catholic priests and nuns actually attracted sympathy from the English. At first, people welcomed the Revolution in France, but Edmund Burke's *Reflections on the Revolution in France* and reports of the horrors of the Terror caused public opinion to shift. In 1791, the second Catholic Relief Act changed the Oath of Allegiance to a loyalty oath to the sovereign and removed recusancy restrictions, allowing freedom of worship and greater involvement in public life. Even so, Catholic churches had to be licensed by the local Anglican bishop and could not have a steeple or bell tower. Parliament might have gone further in providing Catholic relief, but George III would not allow it since he saw here a conflict with his coronation oath to protect the Church of England.

Thus, at the end of the eighteenth century, Catholics were still a weakened minority in England and a weakened majority in Ireland—still second-class citizens, feared and barely legal. Yet the reason for their second-class citizenship had become less clear. England had new relationships with erstwhile Catholic enemies. Spain had been a trading partner since Queen Anne's time, and, although France was still an enemy, the issue was not religion but Napoleon. With the Jacobite Pretenders gone, England had little to fear from Catholics. Had the time perhaps come to remove restrictions facing Catholics from office and limiting their role in public life, and restore to them full citizenship rights?

10

Emancipation at Last:
The Nineteenth Century and Beyond

THE CHURCH OF ENGLAND
AND THE OXFORD MOVEMENT

UNDER THE AEGIS OF THE BRITISH EMPIRE, the Church of England spread throughout the world, appointing bishops in the colonies and eventually developing the Anglican Communion. This Communion is a decentralized organization, with the Archbishop of Canterbury as spiritual head. Members acknowledge one another's rites and consult on matters of discipline and doctrine; but although they must be in communion with the Archbishop of Canterbury, they do not acknowledge a central authority. In the Victorian era the spread of the church under the control of the state led to another crisis of authority and an attempted revival of the Via Media that Hooker, Laud, and Andrewes had promoted two centuries earlier.

During the early decades of the nineteenth century, the Church of England was still dominated by Latitudinarian thinking. Under the leadership of Richard Whately, for instance, the "Oxford Noetics" downplayed the doctrinal in favor of the ethical aspects of faith. They held that doctrines were provisional and subject to change, even crucial ones on matters of Christology and ecclesiology. The Church was thoroughly Erastian and under the control of the state. Indeed, Thomas Arnold of the Rugby School thought "officers of a Christian state should regard themselves as Christian ministers" empowered to preach, and administer the sacraments. Needless to say, views like this thoroughly undermined the role of the ordained priesthood.

When the Whig government in 1833 proposed suppressing ten Irish dioceses and diverting their revenues, a group of clergy and laymen at Oxford University reacted by launching what became known as the Tractarian movement (also called the Oxford Movement). John Keble preached a sermon "On the National Apostasy" that year, and John Henry Newman (1801–1890), R. H. Froude, E. B. Pusey, and others began to publish their *Tracts for the Times*. Even more than the Tracts, Newman's sermons at St. Mary's Church in Oxford, attempting to reintegrate the Church of England, sought to show how important doctrinal truth was to Christian behavior and worship.

The Tractarians focused on what made the Church of England more than a state church, controlled and directed by the government according to worldly standards. They thought the Church should be more catholic and universal. Like the leading figures of the Methodist movement before them, the leaders of the Oxford Movement looked back to the Caroline divines and the non-jurors for their image of the Anglican Church as the Via Media. In doing so, they posed the same questions as the Caroline divines.

- Is the Church of England Catholic?
- Is the Church of England Protestant?
- If it is neither, what links it to the truth of the early Church?
- How does it know what it teaches is true?

Newman looked back particularly to the Fathers of the Church to understand the development of doctrine and the continuity between the ancient Church and the Anglican Church. The Tractarians upheld the bishops as the successors of the Apostles, emphasized the sacramental effects of the liturgy, and sought to interpret the Thirty-Nine Articles in a more apostolic and catholic—that is, universal—sense. Like the Caroline divines before them, they wanted to trace the authority of the Church of England to something more transcendent than Henry VIII's desire for a new wife and legitimate heir.

Then Newman went further. In Tract 90, he argued that the Via Media was closer to Roman Catholicism than to Lutheran or

Calvinist Protestantism. The bishops then silenced the Tractarian Movement. Newman retreated, frustrated by the failure of the bishops and troubled by his own uncertainty about whether the Via Media was a reliable concept. Living in Littlemore near Oxford from 1843 to 1845, Newman studied, prayed, and fasted while writing his *Essay on the Development of Christian Doctrine*. When he became a Roman Catholic on October 9, 1845, his conversion shocked and dismayed the other leaders of the Tractarian Movement.

Without the support of the bishops whom they sought to uphold, the Tractarian's attempt to revive the Church of England could not continue. The interests of those who remained turned more to the ritualistic High Church Anglo-Catholic movement, with its emphasis on beauty and mystery in the *Book of Common Prayer*.

CATHOLIC EMANCIPATION AND THE SECOND SPRING

Newman joined the Roman Catholic Church just as it was entering a new period of freedom and growth. Emancipation had come at last, and it came to England through Ireland.

In 1828, Daniel O'Connell, an Irish Catholic, won a seat in Parliament representing County Clare. The government, led by the Duke of Wellington, proposed the Catholic Emancipation Act and Parliament passed it. At last, Catholics in England were full citizens, able to vote and serve in Parliament and practice their faith openly. Seeing that Parliament would require him to comply with the Test Act, O'Connell refused, stood for election again, and again won his seat. Catholics could not at first attend Oxford or Cambridge, since receiving a degree there required assent to the Thirty-Nine Articles; but in 1854 that restriction was finally removed. In Ireland, Catholics had to pay a tithe to the Church of England until 1869, when the Church of Ireland was disestablished and its links to the state severed.

Emancipation and conversions like Newman's actually increased English prejudice toward Catholics. The potato famines in Ireland from 1846 to 1849 brought England an influx of poor Catholic immigrants, starving, jobless, and in need of help. Yet, neither the Tory government of Sir Robert Peel nor the succeeding Whig government of Lord John Russell took the famine very seriously. They blamed the Irish themselves, considering them to be lazy and drunken. By the time assistance was brought to bear on the catastrophe, one million had died and another million had emigrated to America, Australia, Canada, and England. As in the United States, so in England, prejudice against these Irish Catholics gave rise to "No Irish Need Apply" signs.

When Pope Pius IX restored the Catholic hierarchy in England in 1850, Prime Minister Lord John Russell called it papal aggression. Parliament passed a law making it illegal for Roman Catholic bishops to physically occupy their sees at first. The new hierarchy meant new dioceses—there is, for example, no Archbishop of Canterbury in the Catholic Church in England, and the Archbishop of Westminster is the ranking Catholic bishop. The Church of England did not return the Catholic cathedrals occupied at the time of the Reformation.

Cardinal Wiseman, the first Archbishop of Westminster, urged Father John Henry Newman, who had founded the first English Oratory of St. Philip Neri in Birmingham in 1847, to encourage his Anglo-Catholic friends to follow him into the Church. In 1850, Newman gave a series of talks entitled "Lectures on Certain Difficulties Felt by Anglicans in Submitting to the Catholic Church." He wanted to convince these people, as he had become convinced, that the Via Media was a dream, not a reality.

Newman gave another series of lectures in Birmingham in 1851 on the "Present Position of Catholics in England." His biographer, Father Ian Ker, calls it a masterpiece of satire in which Newman skewers English prejudice toward Catholics and ignorance of who Catholics really are. Nineteenth-century Englishmen, he points out, rely on a tradition of anti-Catholicism while attacking Catholics for relying on tradition. He does not so much defend Catholics and Catholicism from these Protestant/English attacks, as attack the Protestant/English for their ignorance, narrow-mindedness, and old-fashioned bigotry.

In 1852, Newman completed his introduction to the revival of Catholicism in England with "The Second Spring," a homily preached at the First Provincial Synod of Westminster. Taking his text from the book of Isaiah—"Arise, Jerusalem, for thy light is come, and the glory of the Lord is risen upon thee"—he recalls the great suffering of Catholics in England since the Reformation, dwells on their isolation before Emancipation and the restoration of the hierarchy, and calls upon the newly revived Catholic community to fulfill the hopes of all the recusants and enter into a new season of rebirth.

Newman made many contributions to the Second Spring of Catholicism in England. He helped Archbishop Cullen found the Catholic University of Ireland, traveling between Birmingham and Dublin, and delivering the addresses assembled in *On the Idea of a University* (1854). He published several works of apologetics on Catholic doctrine, including the Immaculate Conception of the Blessed Virgin Mary and the infallibility of the Pope. His greatest work was the *Apologia Pro Vita Sua*, a spiritual autobiography published in reply to Charles Kingsley's attack on his honesty and the honesty of all Catholic priests. The story of his conversion to Christianity, his participation in the Oxford Movement, and his entrance into the Catholic Church cleared his reputation.

The restoration of the hierarchy and freedom of religion for Catholics in England, Ireland, Scotland, and Wales did not come without tensions within the Catholic community. The Catholic Church in England was under the authority of the Office of Propaganda (or "propagation," as we would say today) in Rome. One example of these tensions arose after Newman was asked to take over as editor of a Catholic lay magazine *The Rambler*.

Quickly encountering difficulties with bishops over matters of editorial policy, he soon bowed out, but in the last issue under this editorship he published an article "On Consulting the Laity in Matters of Doctrine." Nervous ecclesiastics thought he was giving too much power to the laity. He was even delated to Rome on suspicion of heresy, although he never had the opportunity to confront his accusers and did not know for years of this problem. Other projects Newman envisaged for the sake of the laity, like a Catholic college at Oxford, were obstructed because he was not trusted. But when Pope Leo XIII named him a cardinal in 1879, Newman felt that a cloud of suspicion had finally been lifted from him. When he died in 1890, Catholics and Protestants agreed that he had done much to remove prejudice against Catholics in England.

In 1958 and 1959, the Archdiocese of Birmingham undertook the process of organizing Newman's cause for canonization, but it was largely inactive until 1986, when Father Vincent Blehl, S.J. accepted the role of postulator. In January 1991 Pope John Paul II declared that John Henry Newman had "exercised all of the Christian virtues in an heroic degree," and was henceforth to be known as "Venerable." As this is written early in 2008, news reports indicate that his beatification is likely soon.

Catholics who had been recusants, or who were descendants of recusants, faithful through all the years of suspicion and trouble, were sometimes hurt by all the attention paid to the converts. Newman alluded to this in his Second Spring sermon, contrasting his *knowledge* of their anguish with their *experience* of it. The presence and the needs of the Irish immigrants also added to tensions, as the Irish debated issues of nationalism and the independence of Ireland from the United Kingdom.

Meanwhile the influx of Irish Catholics meant that parishes and dioceses needed teachers, nurses, and others to work with the poor. Catholic religious sisters filled these roles. In an article, Gloria McAdam describes how many religious orders were founded after Emancipation and the restoration of the hierarchy. By 1900, some 10,000 Catholic sisters and nuns of 114 congregations (and residing in 549 convents—compared to 136 before Henry VIII's Dissolution) worked as teachers, catechists, and nurses; with the elderly, the poor, and fallen women; in orphanages and prisons, as well as living in contemplative seclusion.

Several of these orders were transplanted from the European continent, where they had previously run schools for English Catholic girls during the penal years. The French revolutionary government's persecution of priests and nuns had forced them into exile. English women founded new orders to serve Catholics in England, in spite of Protestant threats to interfere with the convents.

Many Protestant religious leaders, like Newman's erstwhile foe Charles Kingsley, believed that convents were sites of immorality and vice, imprisonment and cruelty, as the infamous American book, *The Awful Disclosures of Maria Monk* (1852) described in lurid detail. Nevertheless, the Church of England also established convents, partially at least to prevent Anglican women from becoming Catholic in their desire to live as nuns and sisters.[74]

FRUITS OF THE SECOND SPRING: CONVERTS, CULTURE, AND LITERATURE IN THE NINETEENTH AND TWENTIETH CENTURIES

Along with and after Newman, there were many great conversions in England, which built up the Church with chapels, cathedrals, schools, and literary masterpieces. These converts, mostly from the Anglo-Catholic movement in the Church of England, were well-educated members of the middle and upper classes. Their conversions often shocked the Anglican community, because of their family connections to the Church of England, and their brilliance and reputation. What follows is a litany of converts: novelists, poets, teachers, philosophers, artists, actors, historians, priests, bishops, and cardinals. Even after Emancipation removed the legal burden of being Catholic, these converts risked a great deal. They risked ostracism in their families and among their friends; their livelihoods, vocations, and careers. They brought tremendous zeal as apologists for the Catholic Church in England, inspiring both cradle Catholics and those outside the Church.

One of the converts not connected to the Oxford Movement was the great architect August Pugin (1812–1852). His father emigrated from France during the Revolution and Pugin became Catholic in 1832. He led the Gothic Revival movement in England as Viollet-le-Duc led it in France, restoring and designing buildings in the Gothic style. Pugin's Gothic efforts were more than merely artistic; he went beyond fashion to passion. He believed that only the Gothic style and ethos were appropriate for Catholic worship. Pugin designed not only a Gothic church or chapel but its decoration and the furnishings. He also championed medieval plainchant as the best music for Catholic worship.

With the assistance and patronage of John Talbot, the sixteenth Earl of Shrewsbury and himself a Catholic convert, Pugin built many churches, chapels, schools, and convents throughout Staffordshire from 1836 to 1848. He designed the first new monastery in England three hundred years after the Dissolution under Henry VIII. Mount St. Bernard in Leicestershire attracted Pre-Raphaelite poets, who responded to the Gothic revival.

The Anglican world was stunned at the news in the 1850's that three of the sons of the "Great Emancipator" and Evangelical clergyman William Wilberforce had become Roman Catholics. Two of the three, Robert Isaac and Henry, were well-known theologians and writers in the Church of England. (The eldest brother, William, was not a clergyman, but a failed businessman.) To make matters worse from the Anglican point of view, their brother Samuel Wilberforce was the Bishop of Oxford, Almoner to Queen Victoria, friend and confidant of William Gladstone and Prince Albert. Along with Henry Edward Manning and other former members of the Tractarian Movement, these converts left the Church of England after years of trying to develop and defend the Via Media.

The first great defection from the Tractarian Movement had, of course, been Newman. His retirement from the Church of England and his conversion to Roman Catholicism fractured the Oxford Movement. Manning, along with Henry and Robert Isaac Wilberforce, had continued to champion the cause of apostolicity, harking back to the days of the early Church. In their parishes, they used High Church rituals and were sometimes accused of "Popery." All three were disturbed by the continued state control of the Church, which, for instance, ignored orthodox doctrine in the appointment of bishops. For years, nonetheless, Manning and the two Wilberforce brothers had remained convinced of the errors of the Roman Catholic Church and stayed loyally within the Church of England. Gladstone asked Manning to answer Newman's *Essay on the Development of Christian Doctrine* soon after its publication, and Manning gladly agreed. Further study, however, unsettled him, and he decided he could not complete the task—yet he remained in the Church of England.

Years of study of Anglican and Catholic doctrine and theology, trips to the Continent and experience of Roman Catholic services, and other experiences and arguments finally persuaded all three that the Church of England was not the true Church, that they could not remain its ministers or members, and that the Roman Catholic Church was the true Church and they must become members and perhaps ministers of her Sacraments and worship.

When first Henry Wilberforce and his wife Mary, then Manning, and finally Robert Wilberforce "crossed the Tiber," their family and friends were stunned and disappointed. Samuel Wilberforce remonstrated with all three, as did John Keble, William Gladstone, and other Anglican friends. "The parting of friends" was decisive and hurtful, as David Newsome describes in his book of the same title. "Crossing the Tiber" was a kind euphemism for conversion; those left behind in the Church of England were more likely to call it defection, betrayal, disloyalty, a sin of pride, or a deadly error in judgment, influenced by emotion and deceptive beauty. Indeed, some would sooner see a convert dead than Roman Catholic. The bonds of affection that remained were strained by these hurt feelings.

Manning, a widower, studied and was ordained a Catholic priest. He became the second Archbishop of Westminster and the leader of Catholics in England. Robert Isaac Wilberforce, also a widower, studied for the priesthood, but died before ordination. Henry Wilberforce worked in several lay apologetic enterprises, including journalism. Their brother Samuel continued his rise in the Church of England, becoming Bishop of Winchester—the see of Stephen Gardiner, Mary I's Chancellor—before his death from a horseback-riding fall.[75]

Father Frederick William Faber (1814–1863) followed Newman from Oxford to the Oratory, founding the London Oratory in the Brompton area of South Kensington. In addition to his leadership of the London Oratory, he is known for his hymns, including "Faith of Our Fathers," which reflects on the recusant Catholic martyrs of the sixteenth and seventeenth centuries:

> Faith of our fathers, living still,
>
> In spite of dungeon, fire and sword;
>
> O how our hearts beat high with joy
>
> Whenever we hear that glorious Word!
>
> *Refrain*
>
> *Faith of our fathers, holy faith!*
>
> *We will be true to thee till death.*

He also wrote several books of devotion and spirituality.

Gerard Manley Hopkins (1844–1889) was received by Newman into the Catholic Church and became a Jesuit, after having taken a rare double-first degree at Oxford University. Hopkins lived and died in obscurity after his conversion, and his poetry would be unknown except for a friend who never really understood it, but nevertheless edited it for publication after Hopkins' death. His innovations in poetic meter and diction were truly only acknowledged in the twentieth century.

Robert Hugh Benson (1871–1914) was a son of the Archbishop of Canterbury, Edward W. Benson. After his conversion, he became a very popular novelist. His three great historical novels, *The King's Achievement*, *By What Authority*, and *Come Rack! Come Rope!* depict the dissolution of the monasteries under Henry and the growth of recusancy under Elizabeth. Father John Hardon calls these novels "remarkable for their vivid description of character and expression of fervent belief."[76]

G. K. Chesterton (1874–1936) converted later in life, but his love of paradox and truth was evident in *Orthodoxy*, and he continued to display that love in his studies of St. Francis of Assisi and St. Thomas Aquinas, and his great work on Jesus Christ, *The Everlasting Man*, not to mention the Father Brown mysteries. Along with Hilaire Belloc, a cradle Catholic, Chesterton presented valid arguments against the materialism and socialism of H. G. Wells and G. B. Shaw. Chesterton and Belloc (some referred to them as Chesterbelloc) also studied the role of property in modern society in *The Outline of Sanity* and *The Servile Society*, documents of the Distributist movement. On his part, Belloc (1870–1953) foreshadowed some current issues about the role of Catholicism in Europe in *The Path to Rome* and *Europe and the Faith*. A third friend was Maurice Baring (1874–1945), who wrote a historical novel *Robert Peckham* about the Reformation after reading an epitaph in the church of San Gregorio in Rome:

> Here lies Robert Peckham, Englishman and Catholic, who, after England's break with the Church, left England not being able to live without the Faith and who, coming to Rome, died not being able to live without his country.

The novel illustrates the whole range of religious change during the Tudor age as Baring demonstrates how even devout Catholics incrementally accepted the religious changes of the Tudor settlements.

Baring also wrote a sonnet sequence on his conversion to Catholicism, "*Vita Nuova.*"

Ronald Knox (1888–1957) was the youngest son of the Anglican Bishop of Winchester. He had been the chaplain at Trinity College, Oxford, and after his conversion served as Catholic chaplain at Oxford. He completed Newman's projected translation of the Holy Bible into English. His sermons and lectures on the saints ("The Captive Flames") and on Catholic doctrine ("The Hidden Stream") are important apologetic works. *His Enthusiasm* is a classic study of heresy, which Knox characterizes as the overemphasis on one aspect of Christian doctrine, out of context and proportion, in the search for perfection.

Novelists Compton Mackenzie (1883–1972), Sheila Kaye-Smith (1887–1956), Evelyn Waugh (1903–1966), Graham Greene (1904–1991), Rumer Godden (1907–1998), and Alice Thomas Ellis (1932–2005) each made distinctive literary contributions. Mackenzie wrote several novels, including *Sinister Street*, and founded the classical music magazine *The Gramophone*. Sheila Kaye-Smith wrote a study of Anglo-Catholicism in 1925 (titled, appropriately, *Anglo-Catholicism*) after marrying an Anglican clergyman. They both became Catholics in 1929. She published several novels, studies of Jane Austen, and *Quartet in Heaven*, about four of her favorite saints.

Evelyn Waugh wrote comic novels, *A Handful of Dust*, *Decline and Fall*, *The Loved One*; the great story of a Catholic family and conversion, *Brideshead Revisited*, and biographies of St. Edmund Campion and Ronald Knox. Graham Greene's serious novels, like *The Power and the Glory*, *The End of the Affair*, and *The Heart of the Matter*, tell stories of faith and doubt, sin and redemption. Rumer Godden became Catholic when she was 60 years old. Her Catholic-themed novels include *In this House of Brede*, *Five for Sorrow, Ten for Joy*, and *A Candle for St. Jude*. Ellis' novels *The Sin Eater*, *Unexplained Laughter*, and *The 27th Kingdom*, present the view, as Marian Crowe summarized it, "that, for all our selfishness and foolishness, holiness is possible, that the Catholic tradition is a locus of truth, and that there is a mysterious presence in the universe that cares for us."[77]

The historian and dramatist Hugh Ross Williamson (1901–1978) came from a nonconformist background, and then became an Anglican clergyman in 1943. Finally, he became a Roman Catholic in 1955 and wrote numerous history books. He offered a Catholic apologetic about many crucial episodes in Reformation history, contradicting the Whig interpretation, in such books as *The Beginning of the Reformation* (1957) and *The Conspirators and the Crown* (1959).

Several Catholics wrote books of spirituality: Caryll Houselander (*A Rocking Horse Catholic* is the title of her autobiography), Hubert van Zeller, Alban Goodier, and Gerald Vann. Catholic poets included Francis Thompson ("The Hound of Heaven"), Alice Meynell, Siegfried Sassoon, Roy Campbell, and David Jones. Other Catholic converts who influenced twentieth-century culture were actor Alec Guinness and novelists Owen Francis Dudley and Muriel Spark (*The Prime of Miss Jean Brodie, Memento Mori*). The inventor of slalom skiing, Arnold Lunn, first wrote a book deriding converts (*Roman Converts*) and then became one himself.

Christopher Dawson (1889–1970) wrote influential studies like *Religion and the Rise of Western Culture, The Historic Reality of Christian Culture, Progress and Religion, The Crisis of Western Education,* and many others. One of his essential ideas is that the Dark Ages in European history were by no means as dark as the Enlightenment claimed. He also focused on the role of religion in the formation of culture—and particularly on the role of Catholic Christianity in the formation of Western culture.

The Second Spring produced some fascinating historical fiction set in the Reformation era, telling the Catholic side of the story. As Newman lamented, English history and English literature were Protestant. Catholic authors, many of them converts, addressed this problem by telling compelling stories of heroism and sacrifice. Other than the novels described above, they include works by Sheila Kaye-Smith, H. F. M. Prescott, and others.

Kaye-Smith's short novel, *Superstition Corner*, focuses on a young Catholic woman, struggling with the religious conflicts within her family and community in the days after the failure of the Spanish Armada.

The Anglo-Catholic H. F. M. Prescott's epic novel, *The Man on a Donkey*, narrates the events of the Dissolution and the Pilgrimage of Grace. She also wrote one of the best biographies of Mary Tudor, providing balance and context in defense of "Bloody Mary."

These novels—like Benson's—presented the Catholic side of the English Reformation in an accessible medium. The fictional characters face historically real choices, and endure historically real consequences.

Perhaps the culmination of the Catholic literary influence on the later twentieth century and early twenty-first century was J. R. R. Tolkien's *The Lord of the Rings*. As a work of fantasy, it has attracted many readers to Tolkien's deeper mythical work. The linguistic riches and the philosophical and theological depth of this reverse quest (seeking to destroy the Ring, not find it) are matched by the action and sacrifice of the characters. The philologist Tolkien (1892–1973) was a friend of C. S. Lewis and other Anglo-Catholic scholars at the University of Oxford, forming the Inklings group.

G. E. M., or Elizabeth, Anscombe (1919–2001) debated C. S. Lewis in 1948 and defeated him. She become Catholic as an undergraduate at Oxford, and went on to be a student and friend of Ludwig Wittgenstein. He chose her as translator of his works and literary executor. Anscombe shocked her academic colleagues with her defense of Catholic teaching against contraception and abortion. She protested at abortion clinics in England and was arrested twice.[78]

Other organized apologetical efforts to promote the renewal of Catholicism in England were the Catholic Truth Society and the Catholic Evidence Guild along with the Sheed & Ward publishing house. The Catholic Truth Society was founded in 1868 by Cardinal Herbert Vaughn and revived by the Cardinal and layman James Britton in 1884 "to instruct Catholics in their faith and to dissipate popular prejudice and error" among non-Catholics. CTS publishes inexpensive pamphlets and booklets, and since 1964 has had the title "Publishers to the Holy See." The CTS retail shop is next door to Westminster Cathedral in London.

Frank Sheed and Maisie Ward developed the Catholic Evidence Guild in 1918, including training for public presentation of Catholic doctrine. At London's Hyde Park Speakers' Corner and many other sites in England and the United States, Catholic Evidence Guild members defended their faith. Sheed & Ward produced books by both Frank (*Theology and Sanity, To Know Christ Jesus, Theology for Beginners*) and Maisie (*Young Mr. Newman, Saints Who Made History*), and many other Catholic authors.

In the late twentieth century, Malcolm Muggeridge, Piers Paul Read, Dwight Longenecker, Joseph Pearce, John Saward, and others continued the line of Catholic converts as biographers, apologists, and theologians.

Cherie Blair, the former Prime Minster's wife, is Catholic and speaks often on Catholic issues in England. For years there were rumors that Tony Blair himself might convert. Soon after the end of his term as Prime Minister in 2007, he became a Catholic, with the best wishes of not only the Catholic Archbishop of Westminster but also the Anglican Archbishop of Canterbury. As Prime Minister, Blair at one time raised the question of reconsidering the 1688 Act of Settlement to allow a British Monarch to marry a Roman Catholic. Discussion of changing the constitution of England in this way would have been unthinkable even one hundred years ago.

Blair has not spoken publicly about the reasons for his conversion. Others left the Anglican Church because of the ordination of women as priests. These include members of the Royal Family, the Duchess of Kent (who presents the trophies at Wimbledon) and her son Nicholas Winter, the Anglican Bishop of London Graham Leonard, and a large number of Anglican ministers, like William Oddie, and laypeople, such as politician Ann Widdecombe and Newman biographer Sheridan Gilley.

Catholics and the Catholic Church are part of English society now, although not completely accepted. In the mid 1990s Paul Johnson commented that anti-Catholicism in England was a matter of "a nudge or a wink, a whispered aside."[79] In February of 2006, the English Catholic periodical *The Tablet* reported on 100 most influential Catholic laity in England. These included the head of the BBC, the speaker of the House of Commons (the first since the Reformation), the Cabinet Secretary, and the Defence (*sic*) Secretary.[80]

The historical debate about the English Reformation has also provoked some consternation. Christopher Haigh described one old school historian's reaction to his revisionism: "When I published *The English Reformation Revised* (1987), A. G. Dickens declared it was just what you'd expect from a Catholic—and when told that I wasn't, he expostulated: 'Then why does he write such things?'"[81] Alison Shell, reflecting on that reaction in her introduction to *Catholicism, Controversy and the English Literary Imagination, 1558–1660*, writes: "There is a lingering feeling, among non-Catholics, that Catholic history by Catholic writers is bound to be hagiographical to some degree." Opposition to the Catholic Church's stand on abortion, contraception, the ordination of women, and other moral teachings influence academic reaction to Catholic history, whose "fresh analysis" of the past has not been accepted with the same enthusiasm that has greeted feminist, post-colonial, or other revisionist positions.[82]

Catholics are *almost* accepted as trusted members of English society. The Church of England is still the established church, but it does not influence English society as it once did. The debate about the English Reformation, nevertheless, reveals the issues that remain today, as a result of the majestic will of rulers from Henry VIII to Cromwell and the Revolutionary Parliament of 1688.

Conclusion

POWER WAS THE FOUNDATION of the Church of England—power and exclusivity. Yet, at the very start, diversity and division were obstacles to uniformity and unity, as various factions contested for power from the reign of Henry VIII through the Stuart era. While Henry demanded concord in the church of which he was Supreme Head and Governor, he also kept the Traditionalist Catholics and the Progressive Evangelicals in balance, never allowing one party to have the upper hand until his death. Even the more Continental Reformation of Edward VI's reign encountered divisions within the Evangelical party and rebellion from the common people, who did not want the *Book of Common Prayer* or other Protestant changes.

During her reign, Mary returned supremacy to the Pope, but the brevity of her reign and her marriage to a Hapsburg prince hampered her efforts to reestablish Catholic life in England for the long term. While she was in power, the Evangelical bishops and leaders fled England, fearing the heresy trials and fires, but after she died without a Catholic heir, they returned rejoicing when Elizabeth succeeded her.

Elizabeth, like the first Stuarts after her, faced a most difficult balancing act—really a juggling act—keeping three factions under control. She oversaw the fullest parliamentary creation of the Church of England, opposing both the radical Puritans and the traditional Catholics in the church, in her realm, and in her diplomatic efforts. After the parliamentary religious settlement at the beginning of her reign, she would not allow the further reformation and purification that the Puritan party desired.

The papal bull excommunicating her and denouncing her reign created a crisis for her government and for Catholics, who had to choose between loyalty to their Queen or to their Church. Thus began the era of Catholic recusancy and martyrdom in England and Ireland. Elizabeth also had to contend with the presence of a rival queen—Mary of Scotland—who questioned Elizabeth's right to the throne and fostered plots against her.

The first Stuarts, James and Charles, continued the persecution of Catholics and the conflict with the Puritan party, as they favored the High Church Arminian leadership in the Church of England. Even during the Interregnum, Commonwealth, and Protectorate that followed the Civil War and the execution of Charles I, the Church of England's ruling Puritan party was divided between Baptists and Independents. At the same time, both Anglicans and Catholics were outlawed, yet not so fiercely persecuted.

The Restoration of the monarchy during the 25-year reign of Charles II enforced greater unity for a time, but the English feared Catholicism enough to blame Catholics for the Fire of London and to believe Titus Oates' Popish Plot. They were also tired of Puritan reforms, and countenanced the immorality of Charles' court.

James II's attempts to remove penalties from both Protestant and Catholic dissenters and to create new opportunities for Catholics to practice their faith and influence their society united both High Church Anglican Tories and Low Church Latitudinarian Whigs against him and his Catholic heir. Yet, the Glorious Revolution led to the non-juror exodus of many of the High Church bishops and leaders. Thus, the Church of England succumbed to a long period of Enlightenment Latitudinarianism.

At the same time, secularism was rising in England, as in Europe, and faith and reason, or religion and science, were opposed. In the nineteenth century, after all Protestant dissent was allowed and Catholics were emancipated from recusancy oaths and penalties, the failure of the Oxford Movement heralded the divisions we see in the Church of England today.

The Church of England, as Aidan Nichols describes in his study, *The Panther and the Hind,* is divided into three parts. Descending from the Puritans are the Low Church Anglican Evangelicals. Their theology centers on justification by faith alone and the absolute authority of Scripture. The High Church Anglicans succeeded the Caroline divines and the Tractarians, focusing on formal liturgy and creeds. The Broad Church Liberal wing continues the line of eighteenth-century Latitudinarians and/or nineteenth-century Liberals who were agnostic about the role of the Church, emphasizing the "idea of adiaphora, or things indifferent," noting the comprehensiveness and vagueness of both the *Book of Common Prayer* and the Thirty-Nine Articles. As Nichols concludes, these divisions can make ecumenical dialogue difficult—if the Archbishop of Canterbury, representing the High Church party, negotiates an agreement on doctrine with the Holy See, how can he guarantee that either the Low Church or the Broad Church will agree?[83] Visiting Church of England parishes in London today, a visitor sees that range of theology in practice: some churches offer rosaries and other Anglo-Catholic devotionals and others Zen Buddhist meditation rooms.

In short, the questions asked by the Caroline divines in the seventeenth century and John Henry Newman and others in the nineteenth century still remain valid:

- Is the Anglican Communion Catholic (or even 'catholic'— i.e., universal)?
- Is the Anglican Communion Protestant (or reformed)?
- If it is neither, what links it to the truth of the early church (or does it even matter)?
- How does it know what it teaches is true (or does *that* matter)?

When Newman became a cardinal in 1879, he made his famous biglietto speech, in which he reiterated his lifelong opposition to the spirit of liberalism in religion, which holds that one church or religion is as good as another; that it really doesn't matter what you believe as long as you really believe it; and that ultimately truth does not matter—that, in fact, there is no objective truth (although that statement claims to be objectively true). Newman denied and argued against this view throughout his life as a Christian; for Newman, dogma was essential to religion, and dogma declares religious truth.

After becoming a Catholic in 1845, Newman still valued the Church of England as a limited bulwark against this tide of liberalism, which he knew led to atheism, yet he firmly held that the only true opposition to atheism was the one, holy, catholic, and apostolic Church established by Jesus Christ, with the fullness of authority and truth defended by the papacy and the Magisterium. Newman certainly knew that without the fullness of that truth, the Church of England's position as bulwark would wear down, and it would dissipate into liberalism. That would leave the members of the Church of England without that defense against liberalism and atheism, and because the Church of England is part of the establishment of the United Kingdom, this would compound the secularization of the government and the people of England, Scotland, Wales, and Northern Ireland.

Ecumenical dialogue between the Roman Catholic Church and the Church of England continues, although the July 2008 decision to ordain women bishops will make it more difficult. Both communities are aware of their intertwined history, and certainly regret shared legacies of injustice—the fires of Smithfield and the gallows of Tyburn. Websites for Church of England parishes feature links to neighboring Roman Catholic parishes. The Anglican Bishop of London and the Catholic Bishop of Westminster agree that Henry VIII was an immoral despot when he ordered the brutal executions of the Carthusian monks of the Charterhouse of London—yet the Archbishop of Canterbury's official website lists all his predecessors and makes no distinction between the Roman Catholic and the Anglican occupants of that See. Cranmer succeeds Warham, Pole succeeds Cranmer, and Parker succeeds Pole—from the list, one would never know what upheavals in doctrine and worship had occurred between each of those Archbishops of Canterbury.

Some observers believe that only the Roman Catholic Church can re-evangelize the Angles into angels—as Pope St. Gregory the Great exhorted St. Augustine of Canterbury—and that the Church of England may someday even lose its official state role. Certainly current divisions in the worldwide Anglican Communion reveal weakness, as does the continuing decline in baptism and other sacramental celebrations. The Roman Catholic Church in England has its own problems, however, including sexual abuse scandals and an overall decline in participation—even though immigrants from Catholic

Poland are filling London churches, attending Mass, and asking for help finding jobs and other social services.[84]

In spite of those problems, less than two hundred years after Emancipation, Catholicism in England has survived—and experienced a tremendous recovery. A sixteenth-century priest, shivering in his hiding place as the pursuivants tore through the house, could not have realistically hoped for such a revival; elderly Archbishop Richard Challoner, shocked by the riots after the first Catholic Relief Act in 1778, probably could not have been convinced that Catholics would be as accepted as they are in English society today. Feelings of suspicion may linger—a Catholic still can't marry a monarch, much less be head of the government. Nevertheless, after enduring centuries of acts of royal supremacy, discrimination, and persecution Catholics have regained their rights as citizens, without divided loyalties demanded by the State, able to make their contributions to society while practicing their ancient faith in the Catholic Church.

Questions for Discussion

PART ONE

The Tudor Reformation

1. How does the description of the Catholic community before Henry's break from Rome compare or contrast to your parish or personal life?
2. What do you think about Henry's dilemma regarding a legitimate male heir to the throne?
3. Mary Tudor faced two great struggles before she became queen: the swearing of the oath against her parents' marriage and maintaining her right to hear Mass during Edward VI's reign. How did these struggles mark her subsequent reign? How did they either contribute to or impede her goals to re-establish Catholicism in England?
4. Did Pope St. Pius V make a tactical error when he issued the Papal Bull "*Regnans in Excelsis*," forcing Catholics in England to choose between their queen and the pope?
5. Was the Elizabethan government persecuting Catholics or protecting their homeland security when it tortured priests and laity, and executed them so cruelly (drawing, hanging, and quartering)?

PART TWO

Stuarts, Revolutions, and Religious Settlements

1. The Gunpowder plotters were desperate because of James I's betrayal of Catholics hoping for leniency. What were the moral and practical implications of their actions?

2. How did sixteenth- and seventeenth-century conflicts and wars between England and Ireland influence problems in Ireland in later centuries and in Northern Ireland today?

3. Why did James II's actions to assist Catholics and promote toleration for all religious dissenters lead to the Glorious Revolution? Could different methods or timing have succeeded any better?

4. Was Newman's call for a Second Spring of Catholicism in England answered effectively?

5. Should the provision against the King or Queen of England marrying a Roman Catholic be removed from the Act of Settlement?

Suggestions for Further Reading

ON THE TUDOR ERA

Surveys and Studies

Brigden, Susan. *New Worlds, Lost Worlds: The Rule of the Tudors, 1485–1603*. Harmondsworth: Penguin, 2002.

Chadwick, Owen. *The Reformation*. Harmondsworth: Penguin, 1990.

Duffy, Eamon. *The Stripping of the Altars: Traditional Religion in England, c. 1400–c.1580*. 2nd Revised Edition. New Haven: Yale University Press, 2005.

Hogge, Alice. *God's Secret Agents: Queen Elizabeth's Forbidden Priests and the Hatching of the Gunpowder Plot*. San Francisco: HarperCollins, 2005.

Hutchinson, Robert. *The Last Days of Henry VIII: Conspiracies, Treason, and Heresy at the Court of the Dying Tyrant*. New York: William Morrow, 2005.

Hutton, Ronald. *The Rise and Fall of Merry England: The Ritual Year, 1400–1700*. Oxford: Oxford University Press, 2004.

Moorhouse, Geoffrey. *The Pilgrimage of Grace: The Rebellion that Shook Henry's Throne*. London: Phoenix, 2003.

Biographies

Ferguson, Charles W. *Naked to Mine Enemies: The Life of Cardinal Wolsey*. Time-Life Books, 1965.

Fraser, Antonia. *Mary, Queen of Scots*. Delta, 1993.

MacCulloch, Diarmaid. *The Boy King: Edward VI and the Protestant Reformation*. New York: Palgrave, 2002.

Mattingly, Gerald. *Catherine of Aragon*. Boston: Little, Brown, and Company, 1941.

Monti, James. *The King's Good Servant but God's First: The Life and Writings of St. Thomas More*. San Francisco: Ignatius Press, 1997.

Prescott, H. F. M. *Mary Tudor: The Spanish Tudor*. London: Phoenix, 2003.

Waugh, Evelyn. *Edmund Campion*. San Francisco: Ignatius Press, 2005.
Weir, Alison. *Henry VIII: The King and His Court*. New York: Ballantine, 2002.
————. *The Children of Henry VIII*. New York: Ballantine Books, 1997.

ON THE STUART ERA TO THE PRESENT

Surveys and Studies

Chadwick, Owen. *The Secularization of the European Mind in the Nineteenth Century*. Cambridge: Cambridge University Press, 1985.
Fraser, Antonia. *Faith and Treason: The Story of the Gunpowder Plot*. New York: Anchor Books, 1997.
Kenyon, J. P. *The Popish Plot*. London: Phoenix Press, 2001.
McGrath, Alister. *In the Beginning: The Story of the King James Bible and How it Changed a Nation*. New York: Anchor Books, 2002.
Nichols, Aidan. *The Panther and the Hind: A Theological History of Anglicanism*. London: T & T Clark, 1994.
Pearce, Joseph. *Literary Converts: Spiritual Inspiration in an Age of Unbelief*. San Francisco: Ignatius Press, 2000.
————. *Literary Giants, Literary Catholics*. San Francisco: Ignatius Press, 2005.
Redwood, John. *Reason, Ridicule and Religion: The Age of the Enlightenment in England, 1660–1750*. Cambridge: Harvard University Press, 1976.

Biographies

Fraser, Antonia. *Royal Charles: Charles II and the Restoration*. Dell, 1980.
Hill, Christopher. *God's Englishman: Oliver Cromwell and the English Revolution* New York: HarperCollins, 1972
Waller, Maureen. *Ungrateful Daughters: The Stuart Princesses Who Stole Their Father's Throne*. London: St. Martin's Griffin, 2004.

By and About Venerable John Henry Cardinal Newman

Ker, Ian. *John Henry Newman. A Biography*. Oxford: Oxford University Press, 1990.
Newman, John Henry. *On the Present Positions of Catholics in England*. South Bend: University of Notre Dame Press, 2000.
————. *On Anglican Difficulties*. Real View Books (undated).
————. *Apologia Pro Vita Sua*. Harmondsworth: Penguin, 1995.

Endnotes

1. Pope Paul VI, Homily, "Canonization of Forty Martyrs from England and Wales," *http://www.vatican.va/holy_father/paul_vi/ homilies/1970/documents/hf_p-vi_hom_19701025_it.html*
2. Eamon Duffy, *The Stripping of the Altars: Traditional Religion in England, c. 1400–1580*, 2nd Revised Edition, New Haven: Yale University Press, 2005, p. xxvii.
3. Susan Bridgen, *New Worlds, Lost Worlds: The Rule of the Tudors, 1485–1603*, Harmondsworth: Penguin, 2002, p. 51.
4. W. A. Pantin, *The English Church in the Fourteenth Century*, South Bend: University of Notre Dame Press, 1992, pp. 253–254.
5. Ibid., p. 251.
6. Ibid., p. 262.
7. Ibid., p. 261.
8. Duffy, p. 119.
9. Thomas E. Woods, Jr., *How the Catholic Church Built Western Civilization*, Washington, DC: Regnery, 2005, p. 36.
10. James Monti, *The King's Good Servant But God's First: The Life and Writings of St. Thomas More*, San Francisco: Ignatius Press, 1997. p. 128.
11. George Woodward, *The Dissolution of the Monasteries*, Jerrold Publishing, 1990, p. 53.
12. Geoffrey Moorhouse, *The Pilgrimage of Grace: The Rebellion that Shook Henry's Throne*, London: Phoenix Publishing, 2003.
13. Dwight Longenecker, "The Last Abbot of Glastonbury," *http:// www.dwightlongenecker.com/Content/Pages/Articles/BitsAndPieces/ TheLastAbbotofGlastonbury.asp*
14. James MacCaffrey, *History of the Catholic Church from the Renaissance to the French Revolution*, Dublin, 1914, online source: *http:// catholicity.elcore.net/MacCaffrey*.
15. Robert Hutchinson, *The Last Days of Henry VIII: Conspiracies, Treason, and Heresy at the Court of the Dying Tyrant*, New York: William Morrow, p. 14.
16. Ibid., p. 212.

17. Winston Churchill, *A History of the English-Speaking Peoples, Volume II: The New World*, New York: Barnes and Noble Books, 2005, p. 77.
18. Clare Asquith, *Shadowplay: The Hidden Beliefs and Coded Politics of William Shakespeare*, New York: Public Affairs, 2005, p. 4.
19. Duffy, p. xxxiv.
20. Ibid., p. xxxiii.
21. Brigden, p. 188.
22. Alison Weir, *The Children of Henry VIII*, New York: Ballantine Books, 1997, p. 137.
23. Ibid., p. 140.
24. Hazel Pierce, *Margaret Pole, Countess of Salisbury, 1473–1541: Loyalty, Lineage, and Leadership*, Cardiff: University of Wales Press, 2003, passim.
25. Weir, p. 206.
26. Ibid., p. 223.
27. Ibid., p. 292.
28. Duffy, p. 502.
29. Diarmaid MacCulloch, *The Reformation: A History*, Harmondsworth: Penguin, 2005, p. 283.
30. Duffy, p. 506.
31. Ibid., p. 503.
32. Brigden, p. 206.
33. D. M. Loades, "The Personal Religion of Mary I," in *The Church of Mary Tudor*, ed. Eamon Duffy and D. M. Loades, Aldershot, Hampshire: Ashgate Publishing, 2006, pp. 14–15 and 20–22.
34. Hutton, p. 99.
35. H. F. M Prescott, *Mary Tudor: The Spanish Tudor*, London: Phoenix, 2003, p. 484.
36. Paul Kleber Monod, *The Power of Kings: Monarchy and Religion in Europe, 1589–1715*, New Haven: Yale University Press, 1999, p. 63.
37. Duffy, p. 565.
38. Ronald Knox, *Captive Flames: On Selected Saints and Christian Heroes*, San Francisco: Ignatius Press, 2001, pp. 150–151.
39. Evelyn Waugh, *Edmund Campion*, San Francisco: Ignatius Press, 2005, pp. 56–59.
40. John Gerard, *The Autobiography of a Hunted Priest*, Thomas More Press, 1988, p. 109.
41. Stephen Budiansky, *Her Majesty's Spymaster: Elizabeth I, Sir Francis Walsingham, and the Birth of Modern Espionage*, New York: Plume, p. 104.
42. Scott McDermott, *Charles Carroll of Carrollton: Faithful Revolutionary*, New York: Scepter Publishers, 2002, pp. 35–36.

43. MacCulloch, p. 394.
44. Brigden, pp. 289–290.
45. Ibid., p. 359.
46. Stephen Greenblatt, *Will in the World: How Shakespeare Became Shakespeare*, New York: W. W. Norton, 2004, p. 321.
47. Quoted by Christopher Haigh in "The Continuity of Catholicism in the English Reformation," in *Past and Present*, No. 93, November 1981, p. 37.
48. Aidan Nichols, *The Panther and the Hind: A Theological History of Anglicanism*, London: T&T Clark, p. 56.
49. Monod, p. 69.
50. Nichols, p. 41.
51. Ibid., p. 44.
52. Diarmaid MacCulloch, *The Later Reformation in England, 1547–1603*, 2nd Edition, New York: Palgrave, 2001, p. 6.
53. Lucy Beckett, *In the Light of Christ*, San Francisco: Ignatius Press, 2007, p. 276.
54. Owen Chadwick, *The Reformation*, Harmondsworth: Penguin, p. 293.
55. John D. Krugler, *English & Catholic: The Lords Baltimore in the Seventeenth Century*, Baltimore: The Johns Hopkins University Press, 2004, p. 2.
56. Diane Purkiss, *The English Civil War: Papists, Gentlewomen, Soldiers and Witchfinders in the Birth of Modern Britain*, New York: Basic Books, 2006, pp. 28–36.
57. Ibid., pp. 244–245.
58. Stanford Lehmberg, *English Cathedrals: A History*, London: Hambledon and London, 2005, pp. 185–192.
59. Purkiss, pp. 137–138.
60. Chadwick, p. 234.
61. Adrian Tinniswood, *The Verneys: A True Story of Love, War, and Madness in Seventeenth Century England*, New York: Riverhead Books, 2007, quoting "The Solemn Oath and Covenant," p. 210.
62. Churchill, p. 263.
63. Purkiss, pp. 3–4.
64. Churchill, pp. 303–306.
65. Krugler, p. 231.
66. J. P. Kenyon, *The Popish Plot*, London: Phoenix Press, 2001, pp. 2–5.
67. Churchill, pp. 345–346.
68. Krugler, p. 239.
69. Ibid., pp. 240–241.
70. Gerald R. Cragg, *The Church in the Age of Reason, 1648–1789*, Harmondsworth: Penguin, 1988, p. 158.

71. Ibid., p. 133.
72. Nichols, p. 98–99.
73. Beckett, pp. 341–342.
74. Gloria McAdam, "Willing Women and the Rise of Convents in Nineteenth-Century England," *Women's History Review*, London: Routledge, 1999, pp. 411–441.
75. David Newsome, *The Parting of Friends: The Wilberforces and Henry Manning*, Grand Rapid: Eerdmans, 1966.
76. Father John Hardon, *The Catholic Lifetime Reading Plan*, New York: Doubleday, 1989, p. 131.
77. Marian Crowe, "Unexplained Laughter: The Life and Work of Alice Thomas Ellis," *Crisis Magazine*, October 2005, p. 45.
78. John M. Dolan, "G. E. M. Anscombe: Living the Truth," *First Things*, May 2001, pp. 11–13.
79. Richard John Neuhaus, "A Catholic Moment, in England, Maybe," *First Things*, May 1994.
80. Jonathan Petre, "BBC Chief is 'Most Powerful Catholic Layman in Britain,'" *The Telegraph*, March 17, 2006.
81. Christopher Haigh, "So Why Did It Happen?" *The Tablet*, April 20, 2002.
82. Alison Shell, *Catholicism, Controversy and the English Literary Imagination, 1558–1660*, Cambridge: Cambridge University Press, 2006, pp. 5–9.
83. Nichols, pp. 173–180.
84. Ruth Gledhill, "Catholics Set to Pass Anglicans as Leading UK Church," *The London Times* online (*www.timesonline.co.uk/tol/news/article1386939.ece*), February 15, 2007.

Index